SERMON ON THE MOUNT.

A CONSIDERATION OF THE SERMON ON THE MOUNT.

BY

MAJOR D. H. HILL,

PROFESSOR OF MATHEMATICS IN DAVIDSON COLLEGE, NORTH CAROLINA.

PHILADELPHIA:

WILLIAM S. & ALFRED MARTIEN,

No. 608 CHESTNUT STREET.

1858.

DEDICATED

TO THE MEMORY

OF

MORRISON AND WILLIE HILL:

WITH THE PRAYERFUL HOPE

THAT THIS LITTLE BOOK MAY DO SOME OF THAT GOOD

WHICH THEIR FOND PARENTS HAD HOPED

THAT THEY WOULD HAVE DONE

HAD THEY BEEN SPARED TO LABOUR

IN THE VINEYARD OF

THE LORD.

SERMON ON THE MOUNT.

MORE than eighteen centuries ago, an immense multitude assembled on a mountain in Galilee to hear Him, who "spake as never man spake," deliver that discourse which was to be the exponent of the new faith, and the unerring guide of his chosen people in all future time.

The illustrious speaker looked right down into the hearts of his audience, and read their most secret emotions, their passions, their prejudices, yea, their very enmity and infernal designs against himself. He saw before him the sleek Scribe, the lawless Gadarene, the canting Pharisee, and an unholy throng of every kindred, nation, tongue and people. The incarnate Deity turned away from gazing at the dark and malignant workings of the sinful hearts of the promiscuous assemblage, and addressed himself to the few devoted followers at his feet. "And when he was set, his disciples came unto him, and he opened his mouth and taught them." These few words furnish the key to unlock the casket, which contains jewels of such inestimable value, as to have drawn

2

from the illustrious Webster the acknowledgment that the richness and beauty of the gems sparkling through the Sermon on the Mount, proved them to belong to the treasury of heaven. Using the key thus furnished us by the evangelist, we trust to be able to show that this discourse of our blessed Redeemer is addressed to his professed disciples, and is the most masterly specimen in any language, of close, compact reasoning—the whole sermon being made up of connected parts, as mathematically arranged as any proposition of Euclid or McLaurin, or any demonstration by Garnier or La Grange.

A cursory examination of the sublime address found in the 5th, 6th, and 7th chapters of St. Matthew, is sufficient to show that it is addressed to Christians, and that it teaches them, 1st, what they are to be; this instruction being contained in seven verses, beginning with the third, and ending at the tenth of the 5th chapter; 2d, what they are to expect, shown from the tenth to the thirteenth verse; 3d, what they are to do, shown from the thirteenth to the seventeenth verse; 4th, what they are not to be—not formalists, like the Scribes and Pharisees; the last division occupying the rest of the discourse.

I. Seven verses, beginning with the third and ending with the ninth verse of the 5th chapter of St. Matthew, contain a full description of the character of the true child of God, and show the mode of his conversion.

First of all, he must be "poor," not in worldly

goods, but "in spirit"—humble, meek, lowly. He must feel that he is a poor, blind, miserable sinner, and yet that he has to deal with a holy God, who cannot look upon sin with the least allowance—a God who charges his sinless angels with folly, and in whose sight the very heavens are unclean. How else can the sinner feel his need of a Saviour? How else can he cry, "God be merciful to me a sinner?" How else can he wish to be clothed with Jesus Christ's perfect righteousness, and loathe the wretched fig-leaf covering of his own good works? How else can he long for "the washing of regeneration and the renewing of the Holy Ghost?"

Self-abasement and self-abhorrence must lie at the very foundation of the Christian character. The first step towards conversion must be a deep conviction of sin and misery. They that are whole need not a physician. They who fancy themselves in health, will not come to the healing waters, though an angel be sent from heaven to agitate them, and impart purifying and life-giving qualities. But the Naaman, who feels his own pollution, will bathe himself seven times at the suggestion of a simple child. Wisely then did Jesus make humility the corner-stone of his religion. In this respect, how widely different his teaching from that of the philosophers who preceded him! In their systems, pride, vanity and arrogance, with their necessary attendants, "emulation, wrath, strife," are not only not condemned as vices, but are positively commended as virtues. An able writer* has shown how infinitely superior is the moral code of the lowly Nazarene, to the pernicious ethics of the sages of antiquity. The former teaches "to love our neighbour as ourselves," and that "charity is the bond of perfectness." The latter exalts self, and makes self-gratification and self-aggrandizement the great end of existence. The one system produces love, peace, joy; the other hatred, war, misery. But we go further than the accomplished apologist of the Christian religion alluded to; we contend that humility is essential to success in every department of human effort. Let the farmer be too wise in his own conceit, to consult his neighbours, or read agricultural journals, and it is certain that his farm will be more prolific of briers, weeds and nettles, than of cereals, short-horns and south-downs. Let the physician be too much puffed up with his own imagined skill, to consult the medical authorities, and it is plain that he will prove the most invaluable patron of the sexton and coffin-maker. Let the preacher trust to the illumination of his own supposed genius, rather than to the enlightening grace of the Spirit, and it is certain that Satan will have no more efficient auxiliary. Let the soldier be too proud to study the principles of military science, and he will be but too likely to imitate the example of one of the mushroom generals of the Mexican war, and *place his ditch on*

* Soame Jenyns.

*the wrong side of the fortification.** Let the lawyer have too much confidence in his innate powers, to trouble himself with the ponderous volumes and musty maxims of the law, and the chances are that he will do as another has done—quote the Declaration of Independence as the very highest legal authority.

We have heard a mathematician say, that after a somewhat extended experience as a teacher, he would far rather attempt to make a mathematician out of the rawest country bumpkin, who could not tell the day of the month by the almanac, than to teach the vainglorious malapert, who had studied all the Pikes, Goughs, and Bonnycastles in christendom. Well did Solomon say, "Seest thou a man wise in his own conceit? there is more hope of a fool than of him." If then an humble and a teachable spirit is necessary to success in mere human enterprises, how much more essential is this lowly disposition, when heaven is to be won, a soul to be saved, and a God to be glorified? Many, like the deluded Laodiceans, think that they "are rich, and increased with goods, and have need of nothing," and know not that "they are wretched, and miserable, and poor, and blind, and naked." On the contrary, really holy men are always humble, and their humility is in exact proportion to the justness of their conceptions of the holiness and purity of God. Moses was the meekest of men, because of all mankind he had the nearest access to the great and

* Many of our readers will remember the celebrated entrenchment at Camargo.

terrible Jehovah. When Isaiah "saw the Lord high and lifted up," he cried, "Woe is me, for I am undone; because I am a man of unclean lips, and I live in the midst of a people of unclean lips." Job justified himself when he "heard of God by the hearing of the ear;" but when his "eyes saw him," he "abhorred himself, and repented in dust and ashes." Daniel was so holy that the Angel of the Covenant addressed him as a "man greatly beloved," and yet how did Daniel pray?—"O Lord, righteousness belongeth unto thee: but unto us confusion of faces." The eagle, that gazes upon the great luminary of day, knows best how dark and sombre all else in nature is. The Christian, who looks upon the Sun of Righteousness, feels the darkness and degradation of his own benighted soul. The lark, scorning her humble seat upon the ground, seeks to soar aloft among the dazzling fields of light; but stunned and confounded by the brilliancy, she sinks back with humility and contentment upon her lowly nest.

The 4th verse, "Blessed are they that mourn, &c." is beautifully connected with the 3d. The poverty of spirit that results from an apprehension of guilt and misery, naturally leads to mourning for sin. The awakened sinner now loathes and grieves over that which he loved and gloried in before.

We do not mean to exclude in this interpretation mere worldly grief. For we are taught that "by the sadness of the countenance the heart is made better," and that "it is better to go to the house of mourning, than to the house of feasting." And undoubtedly, temporal calamity, affliction, and bereavements, are instruments to wean us from the world, and bring back the affections to God. But in all correct exposition of Scripture truth, the leading idea is to be taken first; and beyond all question, the prominent thought in the 4th verse is grief and hatred of sin. The promise to the mourner is that he "shall be comforted." God himself will "wipe all tears from his eyes." We observe a wonderful adaptation of the blessings of the Creator to the necessities and wishes of the creature. The necessity of "the poor in spirit," is met with the riches and glories of "the kingdom of heaven." The wish of the mourning soul for pardon and peace, is met with the comfort, which the world cannot give, neither can it take away. Such is the law of God. We find it declared every where in the Bible, and manifested every hour in the dealings of his providence.

The 5th verse, "Blessed are the meek, &c." is dependent upon the preceding. The man who feels and mourns over his own depravity, cannot be otherwise than "meek.* He cannot be turbulent, arrogant, and supercilious. He cannot be relentless, implacable, and unforgiving of the faults of others. The promise to this man is suited to his character: "He shall inherit the land." He shall dwell securely under his own vine and fig-tree. God has made

* Of a quiet, gentle spirit.—*Adam Clarke.*

"even his enemies to be at peace with him." But violence engenders violence, and he who "loves cursing, shall be clothed with it as with a garment." On the contrary, he who is too meek to contend even for his rights, has those rights secured to him by no less a being than the omnipotent God. We meet here again the unalterable law of Jehovah. Men work out their own happiness or their own misery.

The 6th verse, "Blessed are they which do hunger and thirst after righteousness, &c.," corresponds to the three preceding verses. The convinced, mourning sinner, made meek and gentle by a sense of his own unworthiness, will hunger for righteousness—will thirst after holiness, "as the hart panteth after the water brooks." The promise is fitted to his desire. He "shall be filled." God deals with strict justice to all. He gives, as a general thing, to men that which they supremely desire and earnestly labour for. He who ardently pursues the world, will most usually become wealthy. "The hand of the diligent maketh rich." God will "give him his desire," but it may be that he will "send leanness into his soul." The studious generally become learned. The ambitious seldom fail to become distinguished, or at least notorious, which answers their purpose just as well. Above all, he who comes to Jesus with an honest and true heart, feeling weary and laden with sin, will in no wise be cast out. We have sometimes thought that it is this plan of God—this giving to men just what they covet, which gives such fearful import to the words: "As I live, saith the Lord, every knee shall bow to me, and every tongue shall confess to God. So then, every one shall give account of himself to God." In the great day of judgment, every knee must bow, and every tongue must confess the justice of that God, who has given to every man just that which he has coveted and sought to attain. If he have made this world his portion, he cannot complain though that world be in flames. He gained what he strove for. Let him be content. If he have neglected the salvation of his soul, he cannot call God unjust, though that soul be lost. He saved only what he valued; let him not impugn the justice of his Judge.

The 7th verse, "Blessed are the merciful, &c.," forms a harmonious sequel to the 6th. He who has been justified by a righteousness not his own; he who has found mercy, pardon, peace through the blood of the atonement, must feel welling up in his own bosom, pity, love, and compassion, even for the bitterest of his foes.

In the 7th verse we have the first-fruits of the new life—the first assimilation of the sinner to the divine character. In the four preceding verses we have exhibited conviction of sin, (3d verse;) mourning for sin, (4th verse;) the meek teachable spirit under a sense of sin, (5th verse;) and lastly, the hungering and thirsting after righteousness, (6th verse.) The whole process of conversion is here described in exact conformity with the experience of every child of God.

The 6th verse closes with the conversion; the 7th begins with the first display of new emotions and principles in the renewed man. He has now become a child of God, and as the son resembles the Father, so he now partakes of the divine nature, and is prepared to exercise mercy—the darling attribute of his heavenly Parent—that attribute, without which, the smoke of torment must rest for ever over everything bright and beautiful in the boundless universe of God. The exercise of mercy is the first act of the regenerated soul. The whole Scriptures give us no surer test of genuine conversion than is here afforded. We see that the spirit of the new-born child of God is one of mercy and compassion towards his perishing fellow-creatures. That repentance needs to be repented of, which does not lead immediately to the deepest, truest pity for those who are "without hope and without God in the world," and which does not prompt to earnest, persevering efforts for their conversion.

The reward of the merciful man is peculiarly suited to his character. The mercy that he shows to others is shown to him.

The 8th verse, "Blessed are the pure in heart, &c.," is in natural sequence to the 7th. The first and easiest step in the divine life has been taken. The renewed man has now the more difficult task of restraining his depraved appetites and desires, and of overcoming his corruptions. His body is now the temple of the Holy Ghost, and must not be defiled. Every evil thought must be suppressed, every unholy inclination subdued. No outward cleansing by a mummery of religious forms, but the attainment of holiness of heart must be the great end of his existence. He who began the good work, fulfils it to the end. The Holy Spirit is sent to sanctify him, and the pure man has the promise of a blessed entrance into the presence of a God of purity. "He shall see God." He is now fitted for the society of the holy beings around the great white throne, and he has the assurance that he will make one of that bright throng. The highest attainment in the divine life has not yet been reached, and the highest reward is yet withheld. Mercy and purity are his, peace is yet to be attained—the peace that breathes "good will toward men," and prompts to healing their dissensions and reconciling their differences. When this highest grace is gained, the highest reward is given. He who had been merely admitted to "see God," is now declared his "*child*," a joint-heir with Jesus Christ to the "inheritance incorruptible, undefiled, and that fadeth not away." There is a noble climax in the Christian graces, and an equally noble rise in the scale of rewards. Mercy, purity, and the peaceful spirit, are rewarded with mercy, admittance to the presence of God, and finally, with being acknowledged as his child before the assembled universe. Man's ways are not as God's ways, and God's thoughts are not as our thoughts. The highest honours even in Christendom are given to warriors "with garments rolled in blood." Five military chieftains have been raised to supreme power in these United States. No civilian has been raised to the office of President in our sister Republic of Mexico. But, as we have seen, the highest rewards of heaven are reserved for peace-makers. God chose Moses, the meekest and most unwarlike of men, to lead the hosts of Israel. Jesus Christ is the Prince of Peace. Angels heralded his birth with the song of "peace on earth, and good-will toward men." The great characteristic of his second reign is that "men shall then learn war no more," and that they "shall beat their swords into ploughshares, and their spears into pruning hooks." Peace is everywhere spoken of in the Scriptures as the crowning blessing of God to his people. The most cordial farewell of the Israelite to his departing guest was "go in peace." The great Apostle to the Gentiles, who had experienced the rude buffetings of a wrangling world, could breathe no warmer prayer for his friends than that the God of peace might be with them always. Even the turbulent Peter exhorted to "do good, seek peace, and ensue it." There is no sympathy in the Bible for the growling, grumbling, complaining, and contentious, who are ever ready to stir up strife and difficulties between their neighbours.

To sum up the whole discussion in the first division of our subject, we have from the 3d to the 7th verse, the unconverted state—the conviction of sin; the sorrow for sin; the meek, gentle spirit, resulting from a sense of sin; and the longing for a new nature. From the 7th to the 10th verse, we have the converted state, producing the graces of mercy, purity, and a peaceful spirit.

We notice also the correspondence between the promise and the state of mind of the subject of promise. The poor in spirit is rewarded with the riches of heaven; the mourner is comforted with the gospel of peace; the meek has secured to him those earthly possessions he is too gentle to contend for; the soul that longs for a new nature is clothed with Jesus' perfect righteousness; the merciful obtains mercy from the Judge of all the earth; the pure in heart is permitted to see a God of purity; the peace-maker is acknowledged to be a child of the God of peace.

II. What they are to expect.

"Blessed are they which are persecuted for righteousness' sake: for theirs is the kingdom of heaven. Blessed are ye when men shall revile you, and persecute you, and say all manner of evil against you, falsely, for my sake. Rejoice and be exceeding glad; for great is your reward in heaven: for so persecuted they the prophets which were before you."

They are to expect persecution, reviling, all manner of evil speaking. Under all these trials, they are to be concerned about two things only. First: That their lives should be so blameless as to render the accusations of their enemies groundless and false. Second: That a higher spirit than that of mere submission is to be cultivated—"Rejoice and be exceeding glad." Acquiescence in the will of God is a high attainment; but rejoicing, under the afflictive dispensations of his hand, is a grace. Philosophy has reached to the one, the other is the work of the Spirit. The gospel demands more than cold stoicism. None can mistake its teachings. "Giving thanks always, for all things, unto God and the Father, in the name of our Lord Jesus Christ." "In every thing give thanks: for this is the will of God in Christ Jesus concerning you."

Persecuted, afflicted, and cast down child of God! talk not of submission. Uncomplaining Job did not dishonour his Maker, and "charge God foolishly." But the Lord utters his voice from amidst the thick darkness which envelopes his throne, "Whoso offereth praise glorifieth me." Suffering parent! hanging over the couch of a dying child, watching the colour fade from his cheek, the light grow dim in his eye; feeling the pulse grow more and more thread-like, until your tremulous finger can no longer distinguish it. Sufferer! do you then pray to be able to say, "The Lord gave, and the Lord hath taken away, blessed be the name of the Lord"? Rather pour out your heart in thankfulness to God that Jesus has conquered death, hell, and the grave. Rather praise him that your child has been taken from the evil to come. Duty would have awaited him *here*, praise will be his occupation *there*. The child has been called to the higher employment. Thank God for it.

Two things deserve our special attention in the three verses, beginning with the 10th and ending with the 12th. First: The disciples of Christ are to expect persecution under false charges and accusations. The devil and his followers have never yet had the audacity and impudence to persecute virtue as such. They first blacken the character of the victim, and then harass, annoy, and persecute him to death. Jesus was crucified under the charge of blasphemy. Stephen was stoned to death under the same accusation. Paul and Silas were scourged and cast into prison at Philippi, for troubling the city and teaching strange customs. Socrates, the wisest and purest of the philosophers of antiquity, was poisoned for introducing new gods, and corrupting the youth. Daniel was cast into the den of lions, not for worshipping the true God, but for disobeying the king's decree. The Hebrew youth were thrown into the fiery furnace for the same reason. God has stamped so much of his own image upon our fallen race, that history records no instance of men being so depraved, as to persecute the righteous for their virtues, but always for alleged vices. The apostle truly declared, that "all who live godly in Christ Jesus shall suffer persecution." But the godly have always been persecuted as cheats, impostors, and hypocrites.

Second: We notice that Jesus did not deceive his disciples. He did not disguise from them that they were to expect stripes, imprisonment, cruel mockings, reviling, and death. The strongest possible argument can be drawn from this candour of the Son of God, as to the divine character of his mission. When men wish to allure others into an enterprise, they do not speak of its difficulties, dangers, hardships, and trials. Recruiting sergeants, with their drums and fifes, try to allure by "the pride, pomp, and circumstance of war;" they never allude to the hot, weary marches, the dreary night-watches, the mangled limbs, and crushed carcasses of the battle-field. False religions have been ever profuse in promises of temporal well-being and eternal glory, won without holiness of heart and life. Mahomet promised riches, honours, sensual indulgence, and a passport to heaven, to all who followed the crescent, irrespective of their sins and pollutions. The Mormon Prophet promised wealth, ease, luxury, and licentious indulgence, to all who would acknowledge him as their spiritual guide and temporal leader. Jesus Christ promised nothing to his disciples but trials and afflictions. Poverty, contempt, a life of shame, and a death of ignominy, were to be their lot and portion. How then are we to account for the amazing success of his mission? Upon what principle can we explain the rapid spread of the gospel? In thirty years after the death of Christ, the persecution began under Nero. The historian Tacitus speaks of "the great multitude" of Christians then at Rome. In forty years more, Pliny, the Roman governor of Pontus and Bithynia, wrote his celebrated letter to Trajan, the emperor. In it he complains that "the contagion of this superstition had seized not only the cities, but the less towns also, and the open country, so that the temples were almost forsaken, and a long intermission of the sacred solemnities had taken place." About one hundred years after the death of our Lord, Clemens Alexandrinus wrote that "Christianity is spread throughout the world, in every nation, and village, and city." What reason can we give for the wonderful triumph of the gospel in so short a time? It is no sufficient explanation to say that men will submit to any bodily torture and mental anguish to save the soul. True, the Hindoo will pierce his skin with hooks, and tear his flesh with pincers, yea, he will even allow his body to be crushed and mangled beneath the bloody wheels of the car of his idol. True, the loving mother has often given "the fruit of her body for the sin of her soul." The seven times heated image of Moloch has consumed ten thousands of tender babes. The turbid Ganges has often been choked with the voluntary offerings of pagan mothers. But there has always been some notoriety, some éclat, some gratification of vanity, attending the sacrifice. The disciples of Jesus were taught, on the contrary, to expect slander instead of applause, contempt instead of glory. Again, the heathen, who immolates himself or his offspring, not only gains thereby the admiration of his countrymen, but expects to win heaven without holiness of heart. Men will endure torture, ignominy, and death, to propitiate offended Deity; they will do anything, suffer anything, to gain eternal life, except love God and keep his commandments. But Jesus requires his disciples not only to die for the truth, but also to live for the truth. Every child of God must not only hold himself ready to wear, if necessary, the martyr's crown, but he must also lead a consistent, holy, and useful life. This brings us naturally to the third division of our subject.

III. What they are to do, (from 13th verse to the 17th:) "Ye are the salt of the earth: but, if the salt have lost his savour, wherewith shall it be salted? It is thenceforth good for nothing, but to be cast out, and to be trodden under foot of men. Ye are the light of the world. A city that is set on a hill cannot be hid," &c.

The connection between these four verses, beginning with the 13th and ending at the 17th, is obvious at a glance. Christianity is a scheme of active, as well as passive duties. Living for the truth is enjoined, as well as suffering and dying for it. The monk, who immures himself in a cloister; the nun, who shuts herself up in a cell, departs widely from the teaching and example of Him who went about doing good. The devotees of false religion may and do suffer to support a pestilent superstition; but they are not "careful to maintain good works." The pride and vanity of the human heart, the approbation of mankind, the hope of appeasing incensed heaven, may stimulate to the endurance of great torture of mind and body. But a holy life is the work of the Spirit of God. The Prophet Isaiah, (chapters i. and lviii.) had taught the vanity of rites and ceremonies; a holy heart, a blameless life, an ever active benevolence, were shown to be more pleasing to the Searcher of Hearts than incense and whole burnt-offering. The Son of God, in the four verses above, is careful to guard his disciples against the too common error that heaven may be won by physical and mental suffering. This has been the great mistake of heathenism in all ages of the world; it has been the grand delusion of Popery in latter days. The higher teaching of the prophet is sanctioned by "God manifest in the flesh." Cast in the salt of grace into these sin-polluted fountains, (2 Kings xi. 21,) that they may be healed and send forth streams to gladden the city of our God. Let your good works shine as a beacon-light to illumine and make plain the pathway to the skies. These two things Jesus requires of his disciples, viz. to save the world from corruption and to enlighten "the dark places of the earth, which are full of the habitations of cruelty." The salt most probably refers to the inner life-godliness in the heart, and the light to the outward manifestation of it. The influence of both is felt in the well-being of society; the former instructs by example, the latter, by precept.

Light is the symbol, in the Holy Scriptures, of knowledge in divine things, and instruction in holiness. "God is light, and in him is no darkness at all." When the Hebrew saw the glorious light, which he called the *Shecinah*, he bowed his head in adoring reverence. Jesus is "the Sun of Righteousness with healing in his wings." The first words uttered in the universe by the Almighty Being who had evoked it from nothing, were "Let there be light."

"*Let there be light!* proclaimed the Almighty Lord,
Astonished Chaos heard the potent word;
Through all his realms the kindling ether runs,
And the mass starts into a million suns;
Earths round each sun with quick explosion burst,
And second planets issue from the first;
Bend, as they journey with projectile force,
In bright ellipses their reluctant course;
Orbs wheel in orbs, centres round centres roll,
And form, self-balanced, one revolving whole.
—Onward they move amid their bright abode
Space without bound, THE BOSOM OF THEIR GOD."*

As the first command of the Omnipotent God was the evoking of light from darkness, so the last command of Immanuel, God with us, was to "send out light and truth." "Go ye therefore and *teach* all nations," &c. The symbol of knowledge, which the Father caused to rest upon the dark mass of elements, "without form and void," found its realization and fulfilment in the glorious gospel of his Son.

One remark as to the spirit with which good works are to be performed. They are to be done proximately, that men may be stimulated to the same; ultimately, that God may be glorified. Society is so bound together that there is no human being so insignificant as not to exert an influence upon his fellows. The very idiot and madman excite emotions, which mould

* Darwin's Botanic Garden, page 10.

character for good or for evil. "None of us liveth to himself, and no man dieth to himself." The act of A. may prompt B. to do a like act, and he in turn may influence C., and so we may have a chain of sequences reaching down to the end of time. Myriads in heaven may praise God throughout eternity for a prayer uttered before the flood; hosts of howling devils in hell may ascribe their perdition to an oath blasphemously spoken, ages before they were born. Surely, if it be a fearful thing to die, it is a still more fearful thing to live. Philosophy teaches us that not a particle of matter is ever destroyed. In like manner it may be, that not a single action will ever be annihilated in its consequences. If the material be not capable of destruction, how much less so must be the emanation of the immortal mind! Could the disciple of Christ feel in all its force the solemn fact that every thought, word, and act of his would live in its effects as long as God himself will live, he could more readily comply with the injunction, "Whatsoever ye do, do all to the glory of God."

Adam was the great representative of our race—the type of mankind. Just as his sin tainted *all* his descendants, so does the sin of every man corrupt and pollute, to some extent, those who succeed him down to the latest generation. The difference in the magnitude of the results is of course immense, because Adam stood in covenant relation with our race. Still our great federal Head is our type, in regard to the unending influence of every action.

IV. What they are not to be.

A formalistic religion like that of the Scribes and Pharisees is carefully to be avoided. The errors of doctrine of these sects are exposed from the 17th verse to the end of the 5th chapter; their errors of practice from the beginning of the 6th chapter to the close of the sermon.

"Think not that I am come to destroy the law, or the prophets: I am not come to destroy, but to fulfil. For verily I say unto you, Till heaven and earth pass, one jot or one tittle shall in no wise pass from the law, till all be fulfilled. Whosoever therefore shall break one of these least commandments, and shall teach men so, he shall be called the least in the kingdom of heaven: but whosoever shall do and teach them, the same shall be called great in the kingdom of heaven. For I say unto you, that except your righteousness shall exceed the righteousness of the Scribes and Pharisees, ye shall in no case enter into the kingdom of heaven." (Verses 17–20.)

These four verses are closely interlinked with the four preceding. In the 16th verse, the disciples are exhorted to let their light shine. Shall it shine in a few splendid actions on grand occasions? or shall it burn steadily, casting a halo around the jots and tittles—the little matters, as well as the great events of life? Shall it flare like the midnight torch in triumphal procession along the gaudily decorated streets of some rejoicing city? or shall it shine as the sun, "more and more unto the perfect day;" alike over the smooth expanse of ocean and the craggy mountain's lofty top; alike over the desert and cultivated field; alike over the busy mart of men and the solitude of the boundless forest?

The answer is from the lips of Him, who spake as never man spake. "Think not that I am come to destroy the law, or the prophets: I am not come to destroy, but to fulfil. For verily I say unto you, Till heaven and earth pass, one jot or tittle shall in no wise pass, till all be fulfilled." Think not that I will accept your gifts of tongues, your powers of healing, your death of martyrdom even, as substitutes for the smaller duties of every-day life. The invariable tendency of fanaticism is to offset vice by real or supposed virtue. The Mohammedan, with his sword reeking in innocent blood, exults in his pilgrimage to Mecca, in his ablutions, and his abstinence from wine. The Catholic may be cruel, intolerant, bigoted, and superstitious, provided he observes the festivals of the Church, reverences her saints, and is punctual at the confessional. The drunkard often consoles himself with the reflection that he has defrauded no one. The blasphemer oftentimes soothes his wounded conscience with the thought that he is a good neighbour and friend. The thief too, sometimes makes his boast that he has never shed blood. The bold, reckless infidel, frequently prides himself upon the good provision he has made for his family. Thus it has always been and always will be. The world has ever been full of Scribes and Pharisees. Men expect to counterbalance favourite vices by virtues easily practised, because congenial to their natures. Jesus Christ has put the seal of condemnation upon this system of offsets and balances. "For I say unto you, That except your righteousness shall exceed the righteousness of the Scribes and Pharisees, ye shall in no case enter into the kingdom of heaven." Ah! it matters not if the virtues be great and the vices small. For, hear him again, "Whosoever therefore shall break one of these *least* commandments, and shall teach men so, he shall be called the least in the kingdom of heaven." The Apostle James, in the spirit of his Master, shows the vanity and hollowness of that religion, which hopes to buy indulgence in cherished sins by the practice of extraneous virtues. Hear him, ye fanatics, with benevolence on your tongues, and murder and treason in your hearts—"For whosoever shall keep the whole law, and yet offend in one point, he is guilty of all."

Our Saviour begins at the 21st verse to expose the doctrinal errors of the Scribes and Pharisees. "Ye have heard that it was said by them of old time, Thou shalt not kill; and whosoever shall kill shall be in danger of the judgment: but I say unto you, That whosoever is angry with his brother without a cause, shall be in danger of the judgment; and whosoever shall say to his brother, Raca, shall be in danger of the council; but whosoever shall say, Thou fool, shall be in danger of hell-fire." (Verses 21, 22.)

The Jewish sectaries had been careful to draw distinctions between the great and little matters of the law. Some crimes are doubtless of a darker hue than others; one sin is so odious in the sight of the Omnipotent Jehovah that even the blood of his own Son cannot atone for it. Unfortunately, the Jews were influenced by passion, prejudice, the corrupt inclinations of their own sinful hearts, in their classification of great and small vices. (Vide Matt. xxiii.) They instituted the scheme of major and minor duties to be subsidiary to their system of counterpoises. In doing this, moreover, they estimated the external act and not the internal motive—they looked at the stream and not at the fountain. Murder was justly held to be punishable with death; but the anger that prompts to murder, was no crime in their code. Adultery was forbidden; but the roving eye and lustful thought were unrebuked in their scheme of morals. Divorce was regulated by law, but the sinful estrangement of affection between husband and wife received no censure and no comment. Thus their religion was a cold, outward formalism, devoid of inner heat and vitality. The religion of the gospel is the religion of the heart. It teaches that a good tree alone yields healthful fruit—that pure oil alone can make a brilliant light. It speaks of the new birth. It puts into the mouth of the convinced sinner the prayer, "Create in me a new heart, O God; and renew a right spirit within me." It despises the mummeries of forms and ceremonies, and requires that "God, who is a Spirit, shall be worshipped in spirit and in truth."

Jesus manifests the superiority of his system of morals over the formalistic economy of the Scribes and Pharisees, by condemning the malevolent spirit that exhibits itself in causeless anger; opprobrious reflections on the understanding, ("raca," foolish fellow;) censure of the character, ("fool," equivalent to wicked wretch;) and vexatious litigation, (verse 25.) He graduates the punishment of these several offences by their degree of malignity.

But at the same time, with the characteristic benevolence of his nature, he suggests the true remedy to subdue malignant passions: "Therefore, if thou bring thy gift to the altar, and there rememberest that thy brother hath ought against thee, leave there thy gift before the altar, and go thy way; first be reconciled to thy brother, and then come and offer thy gift." (Verses 23, 24.)

Let the poor irritated worm of the dust, when he bows as a suppliant before the offended majesty of Heaven, compare the wrongs inflicted upon him with his own daring outrages against the kingdom and government of the God, who made and preserves him. The injuries done to him will then appear but as the small dust of the balance, while his own rebellion against his Maker and Redeemer will rise up before him as a mountain, with huge and awful proportions.

Our Saviour next proceeds (verses 27 and 28) to condemn the teaching of the Scribes and Pharisees in regard to adultery. With them, the act alone was criminal, but with the Searcher of hearts and Trier of reins, there may be adultery of the soul as well as of the body. God will not overlook that sin which was conceived in the heart, but which was never perpetrated, because time, and place, and opportunity did not favour. The Apostle speaks of those who have "eyes full of adultery, and that *cannot cease from sin.*" 2 Peter ii. 14. "The pure *in heart,*" not the pure *in act*, have the promise that they "shall see God."

Jesus again suggests the remedy, (verses 29 and 30,) "And if thy right eye offend thee, pluck it out, and cast it from thee: for it is profitable for thee that one of thy members should perish, and not that thy whole body should be cast into hell. And if thy right hand offend thee, cut it off, and cast it from thee: for it is profitable for thee that one of thy members should perish, and not that thy whole body should be cast into hell." The wanton look is to be restrained—the first emotions of unholy desire are to be suppressed. The eye (verse 29) is taken as the symbol of that which prompts to sin. The roving eye of king David led him to the commission of murder and adultery. The eye must be shut against the contemplation of dangerous objects, else the hand will surely be employed in the perpetration of sin. The hand (verse 30) is taken as the symbol of executive power: "The hand of God was heavy on them of Ashdod." 1 Sam. v. 11. "The hand of God has touched me." Job xix. 20.

"Humble yourselves therefore under the mighty hand of God." 1 Peter v. 6. "This also I saw, that it was from the hand of God." Eccl. ii. 24, &c. &c. The meaning then of the two verses is obvious. Verse 29 warns against forming impure feelings; but lest "sin conceived should bring forth death," verse 30 exhorts to refraining from the sinful deed that the heart may have devised. But we have also a compound idea conveyed under this figure of the members of the human body. First, in regard to the excision of the offending parts. If the licentious eye be plucked out, there will be one less member to endure the tortures of hell; if the blaspheming tongue be torn out, there will be no imploring cry to "dip the tip of the finger in water," to cool the torments of "this flame." Just in proportion then as the flesh, with its affections and lusts, has been crucified—just in proportion as sinning members have been exscinded will be the mitigation of the pangs of perdition. Blessed be God, there may be such a thing as being "dead to sin;" but this can only be by having "our old man crucified with Him, that the body of sin might be destroyed, that henceforth we should not serve sin. For he that is dead is freed from sin." If, however, the poor sinner have crucified none of his lusts, if he have cut off no offending limb, he will be a *perfect man in hell*, capable of enduring the highest possible amount of agony, torture and despair. The second phase, of the dual idea conveyed in the figure, is that the body of every believer is a temple of the Holy Ghost. "What, know ye not that your body is the temple of the Holy Ghost, which is in you, which ye have of God, and ye are not your own?" 1 Cor. vi. 19. As men are careful to remove all pollution and defilement from a temple consecrated to religious worship, so everything that dishonours and contaminates the temple of the Holy Ghost must be cast away. "If any man defile the temple of God, him shall God destroy; for the temple of God is holy, which temple ye are." 1 Cor. iii. 17. Let this temple, if need be, be shorn of its fair proportions, but let what remains of it be swept and garnished, and made a fit abode for the Holy Spirit of God. Let the diseased eye be plucked out, and the gangrened hand be cut off, so that the body shall be a temple "without spot," if not "without blemish."

The 31st verse stands in intimate relations with the four preceding verses. "It hath been said, that whosoever shall put away his wife, let him give her a writing of divorcement." Undoubtedly, unhallowed love for another but too often prompts the estranged husband or the alienated wife, to seek for the dissolution of those bonds which God intended to be perpetual. There is a fearful significance in the fact, that our Saviour, in his discourse, thus couples divorce with adultery, as effect and cause. Discontented husbands and wives should ponder it well. "What God has joined together, let not" human legislation "put asunder." Moses indeed permitted divorce, but Jesus taught that it was "because of the hardness of their hearts," and that "from the beginning it was not so." Matt. xix. 8. The true doctrine on the subject of divorce is laid down in the 32d verse: "But I say unto you, that whosoever shall put away his wife, saving for the cause of fornication, causeth her to commit adultery: and whosoever shall marry her that is divorced, committeth adultery." Infidelity then to the marriage vows constitutes the only justifiable ground of divorce. Guilty men have wickedly adopted another standard, and have permitted the separation of husband and wife upon a thousand frivolous pretexts.

Again does our Saviour suggest the remedy for this sin—"But I say unto you, that whosoever shall put away his wife, saving for the cause of fornication, causeth her to commit adultery: and whosoever shall marry her that is divorced, committeth adultery." Let the discontented husband contemplate the consequences of his divorce. Should his wife marry again, he must share in the guilt of her adultery, and that of her second husband. Any man, whose conscience is not seared as with a hot iron, must be deterred from seeking a divorce (saving for the cause of fornication) by contemplating his responsibility in all the subsequent sins which will follow the act. Doubtless, the legislatures which sanction, and the courts which grant divorces for other causes than the one specified above, are involved in a like condemnation. We think, too, that it is no stretch of this doctrine of responsibility as taught by our Saviour, that the judges and juries, who, from false pity or worse motive, acquit the criminal in the face of clear evidence against him, must share in the guilt of all his after deeds of violence, crime, and bloodshed.

The connection of the 33d verse with the two preceding verses, is evident at a glance. "Again, ye have heard that it hath been said by them of old time, Thou shalt not forswear thyself, but shalt perform unto the Lord thine oaths." Every one knows that looseness of legislation upon the subject of divorce is a prolific source of false swearing. Suits for divorce are notoriously attended with a fearful amount of perjury. In no actions at law, is there perhaps so much shameless disregard of the sanctity of the oath. The cause of this lies in the natural alliance of one sin with another. The applicant for divorce is tempted to perjury for the sake of after indulgence in sin. This constitutes the grand distinction between suits for divorce and other suits. In most actions at law, property, love of fame, revenge, &c., prompt to the violation of the oath, but in this, *sin is the tempter.* And so long as human nature is corrupt, sin constitutes the most powerful incentive to sin.

The transition from perjury to habitual profanity is natural and easy. Hence the next three verses treat of profane swearing in ordinary conversation. "But I say unto you, Swear not at all: neither by heaven; for it is God's throne: nor by the earth; for it is his foot-stool: neither by Jerusalem; for it is the city of the great King. Neither shalt thou swear by thy head, for thou canst not make one hair white or black." (Verses 34—36.)

That profanity is here forbidden, and not judicial oaths before the magistrate, is evident from the fact, that in the Jewish tribunals no oath was administered according to these forms, "by heaven," or "by Jerusalem," or "by the earth," or "by the head." The word "communication," too, in the 36th verse, ought to set the question at rest. This word (*logos*) could be more properly rendered *conversation*, and then it is plain that the prohibition of the oath refers to the ordinary intercourse of life. The example of Christ corresponds to this view of the subject. He responded to the oath administered by the high priest. "And the high priest answered and said unto him, I adjure thee by the living God, that thou tell us whether thou be the Christ the Son of God. Jesus saith unto him, Thou hast said."

In regard to the sin of profanity, our Saviour, after controverting the fallacy of the Pharisaic doctrine, gives us the true rule to control our social intercourse: "Let your communication be, Yea, yea; Nay, nay: for whatsoever is more than these cometh of evil." A total abstinence from all expletives to ornament or confirm our speech, is absolutely and unconditionally forbidden.

Our Saviour again suggests the remedy. The contemplation of the awful nature of God, as Sovereign of heaven and earth, (verses 34 and 35,) will fill us with too much reverence to permit the vain use of his name and attributes; the consideration of our own insignificance (verse 36) will inspire us with too much humility to allow of that loud, inflated species of conversation that is tricked off with profane expletives and blasphemous phrases.

"Ye have heard that it hath been said, An eye for an eye, and a tooth for a tooth," (verse 38.)

This verse contains the substance of the celebrated "*lex talionis*," or *law of like for like*—the punishment to be in all respects similar to the offence. This law prevailed among the Jews, and the Greeks and Romans. So congenial is it to the ideas of natural justice, that it has ever been found in rude states of society, and is at this hour practised everywhere among savage and untutored nations. Under the name of "*reprisals*," it has been acknowledged and sanctioned by writers on international law. Vattel thus alludes to it: "This leads us to speak of a kind of retortion sometimes practised in war, under the name of reprisals. If a general of the enemy has, without any just reason, caused some prisoners to be hanged, a like number of his men, and of the same rank, will be hung up, signifying to him that his retaliation will be continued for obliging him to observe the laws of war. It is a sad extremity thus to put a prisoner to death for his general's fault; and if this prisoner before was promised his life, reprisals cannot be made upon him with any colour of justice. Yet, as a prince or his general has a right of sacrificing the life of his enemies to his safety, and that of his men; if he is engaged with an inhuman enemy, who frequently commits such enormities, he appears to have a right of refusing life to some of the prisoners he may take, *and of treating them as his were treated.*" Book iii., chap. viii.

In accordance with these principles, retaliation has been almost recognized as a part of international law. History furnishes frequent instances of its existence. During the siege of Londonderry, the besieged erected a gallows on the bastion, and threatened to hang all their prisoners in retaliation of the cruelties of the inhuman Rosen. The threat had the effect of checking the atrocities of that savage commander.* After the execution of Col. Hayne and other Southern patriots, Gen. Greene was induced by his officers to threaten to hang a British officer for every American similarly treated by the enemy. Gen. Washington might have been induced to pardon Major André, had not the army and the country regarded the execution of that officer as a proper retaliation for the death of Capt. Nathan Hale. During the war on the continent of Europe, which followed the French Revolution, we find frequent instances of retaliation. Napoleon, in retaliation for the order of the British government declaring the coasts of Prussia in a state of blockade, published his famous Berlin Decree, prohibiting British commodities of every kind from being introduced

* Macaulay's History of England, Vol. iii., page 208.

on the continent. Great Britain retaliated by her Orders in Council, declaring all the coasts of France and those of her allies in a state of blockade, and proclaiming "all vessels good prize, which should be bound for any of their harbours." Napoleon replied to this by his Milan Decree, dated Dec. 17th, 1807, declaring—"1st. That every vessel, of whatever nation, which shall have submitted to be searched by British cruisers, or paid any impost levied by the English government, shall be considered as having lost the privileges of a neutral flag, and be considered and dealt with as English vessels. 2d. Being so considered, they shall be declared good prize. 3d. The British islands are declared in a state of blockade. Every vessel, of whatever nation, and with whatever cargo, coming from any British harbour, or from any of the English colonies, or from any country occupied by the English troops, or bound for England, or for the English colonies, or for any country occupied by the English troops, is declared good prize."* By these unlawful and iniquitous decrees and orders of France and Great Britain, neutral nations engaged in the carrying trade became the prey of both belligerent powers. The United States, being a great maritime state, suffered most severely, and Congress therefore, as a measure of retaliation, passed, on the 1st of March, 1809, the *non-intercourse act*, prohibiting all trade and intercourse with England and France.

* Allison's History of Europe, Vol. ii., Chap. xlvii.

Napoleon retaliated by the Rambouillet Decree, ordering all American vessels entering French ports to be seized and condemned. This was published on the 23d of March, 1810, and Congress replied on the 1st of May, by excluding all armed French and British vessels from the ports of the United States. On the 3d of April, 1812, Congress passed the embargo act, to retaliate for the impressment of American seamen.* By the provisions of a treaty negotiated by Mr. Rives, France bound herself to make indemity to the United States for spoliations upon American commerce during the reign of Napoleon. But she failed to fulfil these stipulations, until Gen. Jackson threatened to make reprisals upon the French merchant marine.

The principle of retaliation is so congenial to human nature, and so consonant with our ideas of natural justice, that we meet with instances of it on almost every page of history, both ancient and modern. Almost all wars have been waged to retaliate for some real and supposed injury. Wars of conquest scarce form an exception to this rule, for even conquerors have sought to excuse their lust of power and dominion under the plea that they were redressing their own or their country's wrongs. Alexander the Great justified the invasion of Persia as an act of merited retribution for the invasion of Greece by Xerxes; and at the instigation of the courtesan Thais, burned Persepolis in revenge for the burning of

* Taylor's Modern History.

Athens by the Persian monarch.* Hannibal plead the wrongs inflicted by Rome upon Carthage to justify his invasion of Italy.† Hernando Cortez excused himself for the seizure and confinement of Montezuma upon the ground that "the Lord of Nauhtlan had made war upon the garrison of Vera Cruz, and upon his allies, the Totonacs, by the instigation of the Aztec monarch."‡ Francisco Pizarro justified his treacherous capture of the Peruvian monarch Atahualpa, upon the ground that the Inca had thrown down and trampled upon the breviary presented to him by the Friar Vicente de Valverde.§ The righteous Pizarro was but avenging an insult to the majesty of Heaven. The historian Alison assures us that Napoleon constantly professed his desire for peace, and declared that all his invasions of foreign territory were forced upon him to retaliate for the treachery and implacability of the enemies of his throne and his people.

Private feuds and personal difficulties arise in like manner from the desire to apply the *lex talionis* to differences between individuals. Now, when the wrong-doer is punished exactly in like manner as he had punished others, the act is spontaneously approved as one of justice and right. The history of the world and the records of divine truth are full of instances of terrible retribution being visited upon the

* Prideaux's Connections, Vol. i., page 379.

† History of Rome. ‡ Clavigero, Vol. i., page 50.

§ Prescott's Conquest of Peru, Vol. i., page 415.

heads of the cruel, the crafty, and the malignant. The *lex talionis* belongs then to God in his providence, and may be properly delegated by him to the civil magistrate and the executive officer; but when acted upon by an individual in his private capacity, it becomes revenge, and arrogates the prerogative of God himself. "Vengeance is mine, I will repay, saith the Lord." Just here lay the mistake of the Jew. He perverted the law of Moses, given as a guide to the civil magistrate in inflicting punishment in a court of justice, and made it his rule in wreaking his vengeance upon his enemies. And thus he wantonly construed the directions to the officers of justice into sanctioning the most atrocious private revenge.

This points out the relation between the 38th verse and that which precedes it. Perjury is but too often the instrument which malice selects to work out vengeance. What an array of connected sins we have presented from the 21st to the 39th verse! Wrath, lust, profanity, perjury, and malice. We find them associated together every day—the same individual being but too often the receptacle of them all. The philosophy of the combination is simple. Vice engenders vice; sin begets sin. Give the reins to evil propensities in one particular, and they will drag along in their wild and furious career every other hateful and malignant passion.

The *lex talionis* of Jesus Christ is a different thing from the *lex talionis* of revengeful man. Instead of assimilating the *punishment*, he assimilates the *kind-*

ness to the offence. The left cheek is turned to the smiter of the right; the cloak is given to him who has taken the coat; double service is rendered to him who compelled partial service; the beggar and borrower are encouraged in their importunity and exactions.

Every species of wrong-doing is provided for by the *lex talionis* of the Son of God. 1st. Personal violence: "Whosoever shall smite thee on the right cheek, turn to him the other also," (verse 39.) Injury contrary to law and right is comprehended in this class. 2d. Wrong inflicted by *individuals*, under colour of law: "If any man will sue thee at law, and take away thy coat, let him have thy cloak also," (verse 40.) Here we have wrong done by individuals, as opposed to the state, and yet under legal forms, and with a show of justice. This distinguishes the second class from the unlawful and outrageous violence comprised in the first class. 3d. Wrong inflicted by the *government:* "And whosoever shall compel thee to go a mile, go with him twain," (verse 41.) The word "compel" here used, is borrowed from the Persian language. "In Persia, the king's orders were conveyed by public couriers, who had changes of horses at suitable distances, and who were also empowered to press into service any person or anything that might be needed for performing the king's business. The word which expressed this compulsion, was adopted in other countries to express a similar idea." (Vide Ripley's Notes and Commentaries of Scott, Clarke, &c.) The derivation of the word "compel," and its primitive meaning, show that the injury contemplated in the 41st verse is at the hands of the public authorities. Governments were originally constituted for the protection and preservation of society, and rulers ought to be a terror to evil doers. But a large portion of the suffering under which mankind has groaned since the fall of our great progenitor, has arisen from the tyranny and oppression of the reigning powers. 4th. Wrong at the hands of neighbours and supposititious friends: "Give to him that asketh thee, and from him that would borrow of thee, turn not thou away," (42d verse.) The charitable and benevolent are frequently imposed upon by unscrupulous mendicants and unprincipled neighbours. Still it is better that an occasional mistake should be made in the bestowment of alms, than that the pleading voice of suffering humanity should be unheeded and uncared for. The man who refuses to listen to the plea of the supplicant, is himself the great sufferer, unless he is thoroughly satisfied that the object is an unworthy one. He stifles the noblest sentiment in his bosom. He makes God his enemy, and denies himself the privilege of praying,

"The mercy I to others show,
That mercy show to me."

Probably, too, the reason that God has permitted the unequal distribution of property, and the difference of social position, is that men might have the opportunity of assimilating themselves to Him, by their beneficence and liberality. Giving was inculcated as a duty under the Mosaic economy. "Thou shalt not harden thine heart, nor shut thy hand from thy poor brother. But thou shalt open thine hand wide unto him, and thou shalt surely lend him sufficient for his need in that which he wanteth." "Thou shalt surely give him, and thine heart shall not be grieved when thou givest unto him." What was a duty then, is a privilege now. Jesus Christ has taught that "it is more blessed to give than receive." He, too, has so identified himself with the poor of his flock, that a charity to them is a gift to him. "Inasmuch as ye have done it unto one of the least of these my brethren, ye have done it unto me." The Christian, who truly loves his Saviour, can have no higher incentive to charity. Shall he not give freely to the precious Being, who suffered, bled, and died for him?

Verse 42 has, however, as we understand it, less to do with the grace of giving than with the quiet, gentle temper, which the Christian must practise when a wrong is done to him in the shape of a forced gift or loan. This is plain from the fact, that the whole subject of alms-giving is treated of in the sixth chapter, and, therefore, must be superfluous there or here. This 42d verse then inculcates the spirit with which wrong is to be received, when it comes in the form of destruction to property by the beggar and borrower. The Christian under such circumstances must adopt the *lex talionis* of his Master, and not that of a wicked, revengeful world. He must "heap coals of fire on the head" of his wronger, by the grace and cheerfulness with which he gives or loans.

And thus our Saviour has left us (in the five verses beginning at the 38th and ending with the 42d) particular rules for the reception of every kind of injury; personal violence, and assault on character, loss of property, compulsory service, and petty annoyance from begging and borrowing. Assault on character is included with personal violence, for abusive epithets are always coupled with blows. And even the most violent wretch will not strike, until he has sought to justify the blow by some blackening aspersion upon the character of the man he seeks to injure.

Verses 43—45. "Ye have heard that it hath been said, Thou shalt love thy neighbour, and hate thine enemy. But I say unto you, Love your enemies, bless them that curse you, do good to them that hate you, and pray for them which despitefully use you, and persecute you; that ye may be the children of your Father which is in heaven: for he maketh his sun to rise on the evil and on the good, and sendeth rain on the just and on the unjust."

"Our Saviour has now come to the most exalted and final end of all his precepts, to *love* itself." (*Olshausen.*) Here, too, we find the perverted teaching of the Scribes and Pharisees. The injunction to love their neighbours, they had construed into granting permission to hate their enemies, and by enemy, the Jew, like the Greek and Roman, understood the stranger—the man who was not of his own people.

It is obvious, too, from the context, that the word *neighbour* was narrowed in, so as to include only friends, while the word *enemy* was so enlarged as to embrace not only the whole gentile world, but all who were inimical to the Jew in his own nation. Thus it ever is with corrupt human nature; the circle of duties is contracted more and more, while the Scriptures are perverted to justify the enlargement of the circle of the vices. The Scribes had no shadow of excuse for this perversion. They had no license granted to them in the word of God either to hate Jew or gentile. The same Scriptures that taught them to love their neighbours, forbade them to indulge malignant feelings towards their own people. "Thou shalt not avenge nor bear any grudge against the children of thy people; but thou shalt love thy neighbour as thyself." Lev. xix. 18. Kindness to all mankind was enjoined in like strong strong language: "And if a stranger shall sojourn with thee, in your land, ye shall not vex him. But the stranger that dwelleth with you, shall be unto you as one born among you, and thou shalt love him as thyself; for ye were strangers in the land of Egypt. I am the Lord your God." Lev. xix. 33, 34. Here, tender consideration for the stranger is enjoined from a motive that would be most likely to touch the sensibilities of the Jew, the remembrance of his own friendless and desolate condition in the land of bondage. Again, "Love ye therefore the stranger: for ye were strangers in the land of Egypt." Deut. x. 18. "Also thou shalt not oppress a stranger: for ye know the heart of a stranger; seeing ye were strangers in the land of Egypt." Exodus xxiii. 9. Strangers, too, were placed upon the same platform with natives, in regard to legal though not religious privileges. "Ye shall have one manner of law as well for the stranger as for one of your own country." Lev. xxiv. 22. "Ye shall have one ordinance, both for the stranger, and for him that was born in the land." Numb. ix. 14.

Dr. John Brown well observes, "Strangers, equally with neighbours, are represented as the proper objects of such a love as we bear to ourselves; and though there are passages in which "neighbour" signifies one with whom, by common origin or vicinity of residence, we are peculiarly connected, in contrast with a foreigner or stranger, yet the manner in which it is employed in the Decalogue, is sufficient of itself to show that the term is often used to designate mankind at large, with all of whom every individual is connected by a variety of ties. When they were prohibited from bearing false witness against their neighbours, they were certainly prohibited from bearing false witness against any one; and when they were prohibited from coveting the wife as the property of their neighbour, surely the prohibition had a universal reference. The command to love their neighbour, properly understood, was a command to love all mankind; and by consequence, absolutely prohibited malignant feelings—for if we love all our neighbours of mankind, there will remain none to hate." (*Brown's Exposition*, Vol. i., page 190.)

So far from there being any such command in the Old Testament as, "Thou shalt hate thine enemy," revenge is expressly forbidden. "If thou meet thine enemy's ox or his ass going astray, thou shalt surely bring it back to him again. If thou see the ass of him that hateth thee lying under his burden, and wouldst forbear to help him, thou shalt surely help with him." Exod. xxiii. 4, 5. "Rejoice not when thine enemy falleth, and let not thy heart be glad when he stumbleth." Prov. xxiv. 17. "If thine enemy be hungry, give him bread to eat; and if he be thirsty, give him water to drink." Prov. xxv. 21. A comparison too of the injunction contained in Deut. xxii. 4, with that contained in Exod. xxiii. 5, might have shown the Jew that the word *neighbour* and even *brother*, included his enemy. "Thou shalt not see *thy brother's* ass or his ox fall down by the way, and hide thyself from them; thou shalt surely help him to lift them up again." Deut. xxii. 4. "If thou meet *thine enemy's* ox or his ass going astray," &c. Exod. xxiii. 4, 5. Our Saviour proves his Sonship to the glorious Being, who had taught universal benevolence and universal philanthropy by the mouths of Moses and Solomon. "I say unto you, love your enemies," &c. Verse 44 contains the crowning glory of "the law of retaliation," as taught by the lowly Nazarene. It contains *a nice adaptation of kindness to the injury meditated or inflicted;* love is to be given to the enemy; blessing or fair speech, as the word imports, is to be exchanged for cursing and reviling; good is to be done to those who hate us: and finally, when the wrong reaches its climax, and becomes spiteful treatment and persecution, then we must pray to God to suit his blessing to the magnitude of the offence, *because human ability is inadequate to the apportionment.*

Verse 45. "That ye may be the children of your Father which is in heaven; for he maketh his sun to rise on the evil and on the good, and sendeth rain on the just and on the unjust."

We have in this verse the reason of and the authority for the "*lex talionis*" of Jesus Christ. Both are found in the character and conduct of God. *The law which the Father practises, the Son has left as a rule and guide for his disciples.* "God commendeth his love towards us, in that, while we were yet sinners, Christ died for us." "Herein is love, not that we loved God, but that he loved us, and sent his Son to be the propitiation for our sins." "When I passed by thee, and saw thee polluted in thine own blood, I said unto thee when thou wast in thy blood, Live; yea, I said unto thee when thou wast in thy blood, Live. . . . . Then washed I thee with water; yea, I thoroughly washed away thy blood from thee, and I anointed thee with oil." Here we have exhibited the law of retaliation as practised by God the Father. When man had insulted the majesty of Heaven by his pollutions, then it was that God opened "a fountain for sin and for uncleanness." Let every Christian be guided by the "law of retaliation" which God the Father has practised, which God the Son has taught, and which God the Spirit has sealed and approved.

Verses 46, 47, 48. "For if ye love them which love you, what reward have ye? do not even the publicans the same? And if ye salute your brethren only, what do ye more than others? do not even the publicans so? Be ye therefore perfect, even as your Father which is in heaven is perfect."

Our Saviour, in these verses, contrasts the love of God, which takes into its embrace the bitterest of foes, and grants them the genial sun and refreshing shower, with that natural love of kindred and friends, which even the despised publican could feel. The children of God are of course to imitate his example, rather than that of publicans and sinners. The love of one's wife, or husband, or children, or relatives, is only an enlarged species of selfishness. Eph. v. 28. He who is destitute of this kind of love is worse than a brute; but he who has no more extended benevolence, is no better than a publican. We hear much of the cant, that "charity begins at home;" so it ought, but it ought not to begin and end there too. The gospel was first to be preached at Jerusalem, but the disciples were also to "go into all the world" and declare the good tidings of a crucified Saviour "to every creature." There is something peculiarly instructive in the language employed in describing the universal beneficence of God. The all-pervading sun, "there is no creature hid from the heat thereof;" the rain that falls upon the craggy mountain and the smooth expanse of ocean;—these are the symbols and the messengers of the love of that God who does not confine his charity to his pure home in the skies. And how encouraging, too, is it to him who aims at the good of all his race, to contemplate the action of these agents of God. The rain often seems poured out uselessly upon barren heights. But it is there collected and made to descend in a thousand channels concealed from mortal eye, to gladden the parched up wastes below. So, too, the sun appears to waste his generous energies upon the arid wastes of the Great Sahara and the desolate solitudes of Africa, but he may then be preparing those genial influences by which God "makes our garments warm, when he quieteth the earth by the south wind." Job xxvii. 17. Who can say that the effort of the Christian to do good shall ever be lost? Is it not enough for him to know that Jesus has given the example of his Father for his disciples to imitate? Is it not enough for him to know that however enlarged and comprehensive his benevolence may be, still it must operate in an infinitely narrower sphere than that in which are employed these agents that are types of the divine love?

The dependence and corelation of parts from the 38th verse to the close of the chapter, are now evident. Our Saviour after laying down his "law of retaliation" in direct opposition to that of a malignant world, shows his disciples that it is precisely the law by which God acts in his dealings with rebellious man, and then, by way of giving additional emphasis to this law, he contrasts the universal benevolence of the Father with the narrow selfishness of the most corrupt portion of mankind.

Before closing our remarks upon the 5th chapter, it may be well to notice the attempts made by the Scribes and Pharisees to justify vice by distorting the Scriptures. (Verses 21–38.) The image of the Creator has never been so entirely effaced among his fallen creatures, that they could boldly sin without dignifying it by the name of virtue, or, at least, excusing it as no vice. The world has never yet produced a wretch so hardened as not to have some excuse, some palliation, or some authority for his crimes. The duellist pleads his wounded honour as a justification for imbruing his hands in the blood of his fellow-creature. The robber and thief plead the wants of a family, the unequal distribution of property, the wrong organization of society, &c., to justify plunder, theft and murder. The impure and licentious claim that the God of nature has implanted passions, which he meant should be gratified. (So reasoned Hobbes and Bolingbroke.) The profane swearer has "acquired an unfortunate habit; he means no harm by it, and he injures no one." The murderer pleads that "the unfortunate blow was given in a moment of passion, he has naturally an ungovernable temper, which he cannot control." There is too much of the divine original left in our apostate race to permit men to embrace vice in all its naked deformity. They must first throw a covering of fig-leaves around it. Thus we find even in heathen mythology, some attempt made to gloss over vice. For though sin was often and still is deified, yet it has ever been disguised under the semblance of virtue, or, at least, associated with virtue. The Bacchus of the Romans was the god of the vine and of agriculture, as well as of drunkenness and debauchery. The Dionysus of the Greeks was the same being as the Bacchus of the Romans, with the same qualities and characteristics; the Schiva of the Hindoos at the present day is doubtless the same personage, and many think that the Osiris of the ancient Egyptians was also the same. Lust was deified in heathen mythology as the goddess of love, and called Aphrodite by the Greeks, Astarté by the Phenicians, Frida by the Scandinavians, &c., &c. Thus all that is pure and refined in the sentiment of love was made in a corrupt religion to relieve sensuality of its grossness and bestiality. So, too, the Hellenic and Egyptian Hermes and the Roman Mercury, (for they were the same being,) was not only the patron of thieves and liars, but was also the god of poetry, eloquence, and commerce. Upon precisely the same principle, the filthy novelist, who panders to evil passions and unholy appetites, relieves the enormities of his impure tales by a specious gloss of popular virtues. And so we have such stories as the

"Generous Robber," the "Magnanimous Highwayman," the "Benevolent Magdalen," the "Merry Robin Hood," &c., &c. The heroes of the fictions of Charles Dickens have no regard for the Sabbath, none for the Bible, none for the preached word; they look with contempt upon the efforts that the Church is making for the dissemination of gospel truth, and with equal contempt upon the Christian; but, notwithstanding, they are brave, generous, high-minded and honourable. His heroines know not the "power of godliness," they have no love for a crucified Saviour; but withal are modest, chaste, keepers at home, faithful, constant, unrepining, enduring every trial, without a murmur and without a complaint. How plainly does all this prove that men are not yet so depraved as to honour vice as vice, but that they often mistake it for moral excellence, when dressed up in gauds and finery that are supposed to be the adornments of virtue. Thus from the midst of the effluvia and deadly exhalations of fens and marshes, there arises oftentimes a sickly light, which bears some resemblance to beams from the source of heat and life. The pet characters of Dickens would be regarded with abhorrence by all well-constituted minds, but for their possession of these graces, that can only be imparted in perfection by that gospel of the Son of God, which the author seeks to ignore and disparage.

The 5th chapter exposes the fallacious teaching of the Scribes, the 6th and 7th chapters expose the practical errors of the Pharisees in their daily walk and conversation. (See *Brown's Exposition.*) The fact, that Jesus *begins* his instruction with the refutation of *doctrinal* errors, is a sufficient answer to the dogma, so often and so confidently put forth, that "it matters not what men believe, provided that they are sincere in their opinions." Surely, our Saviour thought that religious belief was an essential matter, else he would not have devoted so large a proportion of his discourse to confuting the absurdities taught by the Jewish masters. How, too, can we explain his emphatic warning to his disciples to "beware of the leaven (doctrine) of the Pharisees," if man be not responsible for his creed? Was not St. Paul sincere in his opinions, when he thought that he did God service by persecuting the Church of Christ? And yet he calls himself the least of all the Apostles because of this very persecution. Did he then think that his sincerity excused his wrong views? What does Peter mean by warning against "*false teachers*, who privily shall bring in damnable heresies"? Does he think that false creeds are harmless things? Why is James so careful "to dissuade from being too forward to assume the office of teachers." (Caption to James, chapter iii.) "My brethren, be not many masters, (teachers,) knowing that we shall receive the greater condemnation." If religious belief be a mattter of such small concern, as some pretend, where could be the harm of any man assuming the office of teacher, and how could he receive greater condemnation for his false instruction, since according to the no-creed system, all teaching, however false, must be harmless. The Apostle John is just as decided as Peter and James, in declaring the necessity of right views on the all-important subject of religion. "If there come any unto you, and bring not this doctrine, receive him not into your house, neither bid him God-speed: for he that biddeth him God-speed is a partaker of his deeds." We fear that John is regarded as very harsh, uncharitable, and intolerant, by the no-creed liberalists of the present day. Hear him when he warns against accepting the *dicta* of false teachers: "Beloved, believe not every spirit, but try the spirits whether they are of God." Jude thought differently from these modern liberalists, when he exhorted to "contend earnestly for the faith once delivered to the saints." And by faith, he clearly meant the doctrines taught by the Apostles and Evangelists. (*Scott's Commentary.*) The Spirit of God rebukes the Church of Pergamos for having among its members "them that hold the doctrine of the Nicolaitanes, which thing I hate."

Let men inveigh against creeds, confessions of faith, and formularies of belief, and glory in the liberalism of their views. It is a sufficient answer to their invective, and to their boast, that the Son and Spirit, the Apostles and Evangelists, warn against doctrinal errors, and exhort to "hold fast the form of sound words." When two sets of opposite opinions are entertained, if those who hold to the one set be right, it is plain that those who hold to the other must be wrong. If those, who maintain the non-importance of religious belief be right, the Son and Spirit, the Apostles and Evangelists, must be wrong. It would be very strange, if right views were essential in medicine, law, agriculture, science, literature, and all those things which pertain to this perishing body, and be of no sort of consequence in regard to those which affect the immortal soul, and the interests of eternity. The fact is, that the difference in religious belief makes the difference between the heathen temple and the Christian Church; between the barbarism of Africa, and the refinements of Christendom; between Hyder Ali and George Washington, Nena Sahib and General Havelock.

(CHAPTER VI.)

Having pointed out the doctrinal errors of the Scribes and Pharisees, our Saviour next proceeds to show their actual delinquencies in the three great duties of religion—alms-giving, prayer, and fasting. He begins with alms-giving, since the transition is easy and natural from the beneficence of God (with which chapter five closes) to the benevolence of man.

"Take heed that ye do not your alms before men, to be seen of them: otherwise ye have no reward of your Father which is in heaven. Therefore, when thou doest thine alms, do not sound a trumpet before thee, as the hypocrites do, in the synagogues, and in the streets, that they may have glory of men. Verily, I say unto you, They have their reward. But when thou doest alms, let not thy left hand know what thy right hand doeth; that thine alms may be in secret: and thy Father which seeth in secret, himself shall reward thee openly." (Verses 1—4.)

We observe in these verses that it is not the publicity of the alms-giving that is condemned, but the vain-glorious motive that prompts to that publicity. Doubtless there may be occasions when it may be the Christian's duty to influence others by his worthy example, and induce them to honour the religion which he professes, by showing that it prompts to charity and benevolence. Christ is glorified in his disciples, when their piety is felt and acknowledged. If the good deeds of professed Christians were entirely unknown, great reproach would attach to the cross. Scoffers would say, that the religion of Him, who went about doing good, hardened the heart, and deadened the sensibilities. The alms-giving of the godless and profane would be contrasted with the supposed parsimony of the followers of Jcsus. Thoro may be times, too, when it would be almost, if not altogether, sinful for the Christian to conceal his charity. If a child of God have been unjustly persecuted, and stripped of his possessions, would it not be the bounden duty of the disciple of Jesus to manifest his sympathy by some public act of benevolence that would show the world his approval of his afflicted brother? The true rule of alms-giving, is to bestow our charity with an eye single to the glory of God, free from all vain and selfish motives. No mistakes would then be made either in the manner or the quantity of the alms.

If men did not revolve their good deeds in their own minds, there would be no danger of their seeking publicity for them from a desire of human approbation. This is plainly taught in the 3d verse: "But when thou doest alms, let not thy left hand know what thy right hand doeth." Now, the hands are parts of a man's own body, and the caution is, therefore, a personal one. It is a warning to the Christian against self-adulation. He is not to bandy about in his own mind the contemplation of his alms, as an individual tosses an article back and forward from hand to hand. There is a symbolic significance, too, in the figure employed. The right hand with the ancients was the type of dexterity, skill, efficiency, and propitiousness. The left hand was the type of all that was sinister, awkward, inefficient, and unpropitious. The good principle in man was symbolized by the former, and the evil principle by the latter. The Christian then is cautioned against letting the good principle toss over, as it were, his good deeds to the inspection of the evil principle. If he do, he will surely be prompted to vainglory on account of his alms, or to secret regrets for the waste of his substance in charity. The personality of this verse teaches that the disciple is first of all and specially to be guarded against himself. He has been "bought with a price." All that he is, and all that he has, belong to his Redeemer. There is nothing left him to feed self-complacency. When he has given all, he must say with David, "of thine own have we given thee." 1 Chron. xxix. 14.

The 4th verse suggests a remedy against ostentation in charity. The thought, that "the Father who seeth in secret," is reading the heart, and scrutinizing its motives, surely ought to restrain from the desire for human praise and human approbation. But if that be not sufficient, let it be remembered that God deals with strict justice, and gives to men that which they covet. If his secret reward be their wish, they shall have it. But if they will be content with the good opinion of their fellow-worms of the dust, that alone shall be their portion.

Secret prayer is naturally connected with unostentatious alms-giving. The true child of God is not content with merely relieving the wants of the perishing body. He lifts up his heart in secret for the blessing of God upon the charity bestowed. He agonizes with God for the suffering soul as well as for the afflicted body. The intimate connection between real charity and prayer, enables our Saviour to pass to the second great duty of religion, without a break in his discourse. "And when thou prayest, thou shalt not be as the hypocrites are; for they love to pray standing in the synagogues, and in the corners of the streets, that they may be seen of men. Verily, I say unto you, They have their reward.

But thou, when thou prayest, enter into thy closet, and when thou hast shut thy door, pray to thy Father which is in secret; and thy Father, which seeth in secret, shall reward thee openly. But when ye pray, use not vain repetitions, as the heathen do: for they think that they shall be heard for their much speaking. Be not ye therefore like unto them: for your Father knoweth what things ye have need of before ye ask him." (Verses 5—8.)

Our Saviour passes in these verses, by a natural transition, from the perception by the omniscient Eye of the smallest mite given in secret from pure motives, to the hearing by the omniscient Ear of the softest sigh of the burdened heart, the mere breathing of the soul after God. Lam. iii. 56. He passes naturally from speaking of the hypocrisy that seeks glory from men by ostentatious charity, to the hypocrisy that wins praise from a worm of the dust, by a mockery of worship of the great God of heaven.

We observe that prayer is not enjoined as a new duty, but spoken of as one already known and acknowledged. "And when ye pray, &c." Prayer is in fact a necessity of our being. All men feel its obligation—the Pagan and the Papist, the Mahommedan and the Mormon, alike with the Christian. The sage feels his darkness and ignorance as strongly as the drivelling idiot. The warrior, in the midst of his legions and cohorts, feels his helplessness as much as the unarmed peasant. Even the bold blasphemer will "call earnestly upon God in the day of trouble."

Men may "set at nought all his counsel, and have none of his reproof," in time of health and prosperity. But they will cry aloud "when their fear cometh as a desolation, and their destruction as a whirlwind." Who ever scoffed at prayer on a vessel foundering at sea? Who ever was ashamed to lift up his voice to the omnipotent One, when he knew "that his heart and flesh were failing"? "Men may live fools, but fools they cannot die." "As I live, saith the Lord, every knee shall bow to me, and every tongue shall confess to God." It is the law of God, we cannot set it aside. We must either "pray in an acceptable time" of our own free will, or God will force us to pray, when he "will laugh at our calamity, and mock when our fear cometh." Let us be wise, and pray to him when all is well with us; lest he be angry, and "cover himself with a cloud that our prayer should not pass through," when we call upon him in the extremity of our distress.

Two things are forbidden and one enjoined, in the verses above quoted. Praying "to be seen of men," and the use of vain repetitions in prayer are positively prohibited. Withdrawment from the world—retirement to the closet of his own heart, to the secret recesses of his own soul, is emphatically comcommanded.

It may be well to remark, that our Saviour does not forbid public prayer, where the motive is not the praise of man; neither does he forbid repetitions that are not vain. In regard to public prayer, we have the examples of the holy men of both dispensations, the Mosaic and the Christian. Elijah prayed in the presence of immense multitudes of people, that the fire of God might descend and consume the sacrafice, so that the priests of Baal might be confounded, and the true God be acknowledged. 1 Kings xviii. 36, 37. David's prayer for Solomon and his people, was uttered "before all the congregation." 1 Chron. xxix. 10—19. At the dedication of the temple, Solomon "kneeled down upon his knees before all the congregation of Israel, and spread forth his hands toward heaven, and said, &c." 2 Chron. vi. 13—42. Ezra read and expounded the law in presence of all the people, and then worshipped God. Neh. viiii. 5, 6. When Nehemiah had convoked a solemn assembly, they read one fourth part of the day out of the book of the law, and one fourth part they confessed their sins, and worshipped the Lord their God. Neh. ix. 3. The incense and burnt-offering of the Jews, were, in fact, only forms of public worship. Our Saviour himself prayed in the presence of all his disciples on the way to Gethsemane; his prayer of agony in the garden was before Peter, and James, and John; his cry of anguish on the cross was uttered in the hearing of the savage host around him. Stephen "kneeled down, and cried with a loud voice, Lord, lay not this sin to their charge," when the murderous shower of stones was falling upon him. Public prayer was offered by the Apostles at the time of the choosing of Matthias. The assembly of believers were engaged in public prayer, when "they were all filled with the Holy Ghost." Acts iv. 31. Paul kneeled down and prayed with the elders of Ephesus; he prayed also in the presence of "the whole ship's company," when the vessel was about to be cast away. These few examples are sufficient to show that public prayer is a divinely appointed ordinance, and therefore not prohibited in the verses under consideration. Nor are earnest repetitions in prayer forbidden. The two blind men by the wayside prevailed with their one and oft repeated cry, "Have mercy on us, O Lord, thou son of David." Matt. xx. 30, 31. Jesus himself used the same words three times in his agony in the garden. Matt. xxvi. 44. It is remarkable that the longest chapter in the Bible (119th psalm) contains a tribute in almost every verse to the excellency of the Scriptures, under the various names of law, testimony, statutes, word, judgments, precepts, and commandments. The prayer too, "teach me thy statutes," is repeated in it no less than seven times. In the 136th psalm, the words, "His mercy endureth for ever," occur twenty-six times. In Daniel's prayer for the restoration of Israel, he repeated the word "hear" four times. Our Saviour then does not condemn repetition *per se*, but that repetition which claims merit because of its much speaking. Such as that of the priests of Baal, when they cried all day, "O Baal hear us." Such as that of the priests of Bhud, who spend whole days in repeating the sacred word "Um." Such as that of the Mohammedans, when they cry for hours the single word "Alla." Such as that of the Romish worshippers, who repeat the same salutations to the Virgin over and over again. In a Catholic book of devotions, in our possession, almost every sentence closes with "Ave Maria." "It is curious to observe the identity of character of false religion in all its forms—heathenism, corrupted Judaism, and corrupted Christianity. The poor deluded Romanists are in the habit of repeating the Lord's prayer and the salutations of the Virgin in a language they do not understand; and of expecting that by the frequent repetition of these, which they number by counting a string of beads, they are to obtain deliverance from the greatest evils, and the possession of the most important blessings." (See *Brown's Exposition*, vol. i. page 208.) We learn from the missionary Huc, that the Tartars have an improvement upon the Romish rosary or string of beads. They have a revolving disc, turned by the wind, every revolution of which counts a prayer. All these prayers are, of course, as near alike to one another as may be. In point of economy of time, and similarity of character, they are superior to the "Ave Marias" of Popery.

Ostentatious public prayer and vain repetitions in prayer proceed from the same source—a low conception of the awful character of God. He who has just views in regard to the august majesty of the Most High, can never insult him by pompous declamation in prayer, nor by a hypocritical worship of him in public, to gain the applause of his fellow-creatures. He who has contrasted the purity of God with his own vileness, can never be so vain and foolish as to think that a mummery of words, how oft soever repeated, can appear meritorious in the eyes of the Holy Being, who sees uncleanness in the very heavens.

Our Saviour, then, suggests the true remedy for these gross perversions of prayer—"Enter into thy closet, and when thou hast shut thy door, pray to thy Father which is in secret." We understand by these words more than the mere direction to retire from the public gaze. The monk and the nun may count their beads in the darkness of their cells. The Tartar may whirl his praying circle in the solitude of his boundless steppes of the wilderness. The profoundest silence and deepest retirement may bring no exalted ideas of God. Privacy may favour, but can never produce a devotional spirit. That is the gift of the Holy Spirit, and is independent of locality. Blind Bartimeus was heard by the way-side, but God turned a deaf ear to the prayer of the boastful Pharisee, though it was uttered in the temple of the Most High. Luke xviii. 11.

By entering the closet then, we understand not merely exclusion from the world, but withdrawal from worldly thoughts, and musing upon the character of God until the fire burn. Privacy is doubtless favourable to a devout frame of mind, but there may be as much irreverence in the cloisters of monasteries, as in the market-places of cities. But the example of our Saviour, who chose the night-season and the solitude of the mountain for his devotions, is sufficient to show the necessity of an occasional withdrawal from the noise and bustle of the world, to commune alone with the Father of our spirits. Secret prayer assimilates the believer to God. "'Tis the glory of God to conceal a thing." "The secret things belong unto the Lord our God." "Clouds and darkness are round about Him." It is the glorious privilege of the child of God to commune in secret with this awful and mysterious Being, and thus "to be changed into his image." "The heart," too, alone "knows its own bitterness," and can only be unburdened in secret to Him, who "is touched with the feeling of our infirmities." We are invited to cast *all* our cares upon him, but there are many cares that can only be cast upon him in secret prayer. We would prefer to be alone at such times, but if that be impossible, secret prayer, acceptable to the Father, who seeth in secret, can be offered, like Nehemiah's, in the very audience-chamber of the king, or like Hannah's, in the courts of the temple. The believer, in secret communing with God, makes the nearest approach that ever can be attained in this vale of tears to realizing the wish of Moses, "I beseech thee, show me thy glory." Exod. xxxiii. 18. God revealed himself in an especial manner to Moses in the solitude of Sinai; and he spoke to Elijah as a man speaketh to his friend, when he stood alone in the same desert place. 1 Kings xix. 12.

But the angel Gabriel was "caused to fly swiftly," in answer to the prayer of Daniel, offered amidst the splendour and tumult of Shusan, the palace. God looks at the withdrawal of the heart and not of the body, from the noise and bustle of the world. The command to "pray always," implies that the heart may be lifted up in secret devotion amidst the most pressing duties of active life. Still, all should have and all might have special seasons of private prayer. Colonel Gardiner could find such seasons amidst the exciting scenes of civil war and domestic dissension. Washington could find such, on his most arduous and active campaigns. David could find such, even when hunted down by his enemies like a wild beast of the wilderness. Above all, the Son of God, when engaged in his glorious mission on earth, could find time to spend whole nights in secret prayer. No man can say that he is more diligently or more usefully employed than were Gardiner, Washington, David, and our blessed Redeemer. Let no one then dare to say that he has no time for secret prayer.

One word in regard to the length of public prayers. The 8th verse condemns all windy, verbose supplications, all rhetorical flourishes, all pompous declamation, all attempts to tickle the ear and please the fancy of a creature of the dust, whilst addressing the awful Majesty of Heaven. How offensive must it be to the Searcher of hearts to listen to a poor, guilty, dependent sinner, breathing the language of reverence and penitence, and yet at the same time exulting in the supposed eloquence, or pathos, or learning, of his penitential prayer. But even a truly devout prayer in public should not be so long, as to weary and distract the attention of the audience. "God is in heaven, and thou upon earth; therefore let thy words be few. For a dream cometh through the multitude of business; and a fool's voice is known by multitude of words." Eccles. v. 2, 3. Scott has the following judicious observations on this passage. "These verbose supplications show indisputable traces of a man's ignorance and folly, and that he has confused, false, and dishonourable thoughts of God and religion: even as the incoherencies of a dream often show the multitude of schemes, anxieties, and employments which employ men's waking hours, and the prevalent disposition of their minds and hearts." (*Commentary*, vol. ii.) Our Saviour spent whole nights in prayer, but it was when alone upon the mountain's top. "The Lord save me, or I perish" of sinking Peter, and the "God be merciful to me a sinner," of the poor Publican, may reach the ears of the Lord of Sabaoth, when he will turn away with abhorrence from the bombastic jargon that sometimes disgraces our pulpits.

THE LORD'S PRAYER.

"After this manner therefore pray ye: Our Father which art in heaven, hallowed be thy name. Thy kingdom come. Thy will be done in earth as it is in heaven. Give us this day our daily bread: and forgive us our debts, as we forgive our debtors. And lead us not into temptation, but deliver us from evil. For thine is the kingdom, and the power, and the glory, for ever. Amen. (Verses 9–13.)

This wonderful prayer has excited the admiration of the wise and good throughout the world, from its delivery to the present hour. Even the stupid infidel and shallow scoffer have not failed to perceive its beauty, sublimity and comprehensiveness. It has been made the study of so many holy men, and the theme of so many able pens, that we will only presume to give a brief analysis, and notice a few points.

It is a sacred triad—for it embraces the three elements of prayer—invocation, supplication, and thanksgiving. It consists of three parts. 1st. What relates to the glory of God. 2d. What is required for the temporal and spiritual well-being of man. 3d. Doxology, or ascription of praise to the Triune God. These three parts are again subdivided into three sections; the first two containing each three petitions, and the last giving the three ascriptions of kingdom, power, and glory to the Trinity. In each of the three petitions in the first two sections, there are three objects of consideration. Thus in the first, we have a name, God's name, and we pray that it may be hallowed. "Name," "God," and "hallowed" are then the three objects under consideration. In the second petition, they are, "thy," "kingdom," and "come." In the third, "thy," "will," and "be done." In the fourth, "daily bread," "give," and "us." In the fifth, "forgive," "us," and "debts." In the sixth, "lead not," "us," and "temptation;" or taking the converse of the petition, they are "deliver," "us," and "evil." The prayer, too, in its very language presupposes the existence in the heart of the utterer, of the three cardinal graces of the Christian character—Faith, Hope, and Charity.

Faith. For he says "Our Father." "He that cometh to God must believe that he is, and that he is a rewarder of them that diligently seek him." Heb. xi. 6.

Hope. For he uses the language of expectation, "May thy kingdom with all its blessings come. May my daily food be given," &c.

Charity—Love to God and love to man. For he uses a sublime ascription of praise to the Triune God, and he asks only for pardon from God, upon condition of his own universal good-will to his fellow-creatures. "Forgive me my debts, as I forgive my debtors."

We regard then the whole prayer as teaching, or rather acknowledging, the doctrine of the Trinity, by its form, structure, and phraseology. It is a sublime hymn of praise to the three persons and one essence in the mysterious Godhead. It seems to us that the petitions and the doxology are addressed to different persons in the glorious Trinity. Thus we pray that the great name of God the Father may be hallowed; that the kingdom of Christ may come; and that the will, the holy will of the Holy Spirit may be done. We pray that the Father of our spirits may give us food for our bodies; that the Son, who has taken the penalty of our debts upon himself, may forgive these debts; and that the Spirit of truth, whom Christ had promised, may "guide us into all truth," (John xvi. 13,) and lead us out of the paths of sin and temptation. We understand the "kingdom" in the doxology to be different from the "kingdom" in the second petition. In the petition it evidently refers to the reign of Christ, to the triumph of the gospel of grace. But in the doxology, it is an ascription of absolute sovereignty to God the Father, and employed in the same sense as in 1 Chron. xxix. 11, "Thine is the kingdom, O Lord, and thou art exalted as head above all." Again, in Daniel vii. 27, "And the kingdom and dominion, and the greatness of the kingdom under the whole heaven, shall be given to the saints of the Most High, whose kingdom is an everlasting kingdom, and all dominions shall serve and obey him." Nothing can be plainer than that God the Father is the august personage referred to in this verse, and that the word "kingdom" is employed to convey the idea of his absolute and unconditional control over the universe. We understand then the "kingdom," or absolute sovereignty, to be ascribed in the doxology to God the Father, while the "power" is ascribed to the Son, and the "glory" to the Holy Spirit. In the New Testament, "power" is the most common attribute of the Son. "That the power of Christ may rest upon me." 2 Cor. xii. 9. "That I may know him, and the power of his resurrection." Philip. iii. 10.

"Until the appearing of our Lord Jesus Christ . . . . . to whom be honour and power everlasting, Amen." 1 Tim. vi. 14–16. "And I heard a loud voice in heaven, saying, Now is come salvation, and strength, and the kingdom of our God, and the power of his Christ." Rev. xii. 10. This verse ascribes the kingdom to God the Father, and the power to Christ, just as we find it in the doxology. The angels around the throne, whom John saw in his vision, cried with a loud voice, "Worthy is the Lamb that was slain to receive *power*, and riches, and wisdom, and strength," &c. Christ himself said, "All power is given unto me in heaven and in earth." Matt. xxviii. 18.

To show that glory is an ascription of praise to the Holy Spirit, it is sufficient to prove that the glory of God is manifested specially by the work of sanctification, which is the office of the Spirit. "Herein is my Father glorified, that ye bear much fruit." John xv. 8. Our Saviour here declares that God is glorified by the fruits of the Spirit. "And whom he justified, them he also glorified." Rom. viii. 30. Glorification and sanctification are here used as synonymous terms. "When he shall come to be glorified in his saints and admired in all them that believe." 2 Thess. i. 10. The crown of glory of our Saviour in the great day of judgment, is to be his sanctified believers. "So have I caused the whole house of Israel and the whole house of Judah to cleave unto me; that they might be unto me for a people, and for a name, and for a praise, and for a glory." Jer. xiii. 11. Here God declares that his sanctified people are his glory and his praise. "Being filled with the fruits of righteousness, which are by Jesus Christ, unto the glory and praise of God." Philip. i. 11. "By righteousness, we understand the whole work of the Spirit of God in the soul of the believer." (*Clarke.*) The fruits of this righteousness the believer received a title to by the death of his Redeemer, but they were matured in his soul by the genial influences of the Spirit. "For the Spirit of glory and of God resteth upon you." 1 Pet. iv. 14. The Holy Ghost is in this verse called the Spirit of Glory, and he is said to rest upon the believer, as he rested upon Christ at his baptism. As the glory of the Triune God results specially from the work of sanctification, it is right that the ascription of glory should specially be given to the Spirit that sanctifies.

A more critical examination of the Lord's Prayer will confirm the view, that it recognizes the doctrine of the Trinity. The first petition, "Hallowed be thy name," is certainly addressed to God the Father. "Name," as a title, is applied in the Old Testament Scriptures specially to the Father. "That thou mayest fear this glorious and fearful name, THE LORD, THY GOD." Deut. xxviii. 58. "For in the Lord JEHOVAH is everlasting strength . . . . the desire of our soul is to thy name, and to the remembrance of thee." Isaiah xxvi. 4–8. "And they shall say unto me, What is his name? What shall I say unto them? And God said unto Moses, I AM THAT I AM." Exod.

iii. 13, 14. See also Ps. xxix. 2, xxiv. 3, lxi. 5, &c. We may here remark, that the application of the word "name" to Christ, in the sense of "any thing by which he makes himself known," is to our mind a most conclusive proof of his divinity. "In his name shall the gentiles trust;" "believing, you might have life through his name;" "and for my name's sake has laboured;" "thou holdest fast my name;" "in thy name have we cast out devils;" "let every one that nameth the name of Christ depart from iniquity," &c.

In the invocation, "Our Father, who art in heaven," the word "heaven" in the original Greek is plural, (*tou tois,*) the heavens, or universe. Whereas in the third petition, (thy will be done on earth as it is in heaven,) the word "heaven" is singular, (*touto,*) and means the place "where his honour dwells"—the local habitation of angels and glorified spirits. These distinctions in number have been observed in the Vulgate and in the French copies of the New Testament. But from specimens before us, of the Lord's Prayer in most of the modern languages in Europe, we infer that the different words employed in the original Greek have not been generally noticed. The distinction gives a peculiar beauty and emphasis to the third petition. We pray that the will of God may be done, even on this vile earth, as it is around the Great White Throne—where angelic beings and glorified believers behold him face to face.

The word "hallowed" is a compound in the original, and signifies literally "not of the earth."* The

* Adam Clarke.

earth is, in its very nature, polluted. Its touch defiles and contaminates whatever is clean and pure. It was made to be trodden under foot of him, who was formed in the image of God. And yet he, as a creature of the dust, is, from his very bodily organization, corrupt and debased. "He that is of the earth is earthy." "Who can bring a clean thing out of an unclean?" "How can he be clean that is born of woman?" Even the "wisdom" of the poor fallen wretch, "is earthly, sensual, devilish." How then can this worm of the earth justify himself before God? Can he do it by external rites and ceremonies? Do we not pray that God's name may be hallowed by being removed from earthly taint and tarnish? All lip-service, all hypocritical genuflexions, all mummeries of worship, where the heart is not engaged, are mere bodily exercises, and are therefore, like the body, full of all rottenness and uncleanness. We pray that God's name may be removed from all this impurity. This prayer then contains the most complete refutation of the absurd doctrine, that men can work out their own salvation. Man is of the earth and his deeds are earthy. The stream cannot rise higher than the fountain. All outward acts of piety, alms-giving, prayer and fasting, are of the perishing body, and must perish with it. The Holy Spirit can alone fit the immortal part for the society of God and holy beings. "God is a Spirit, and must be worshipped in spirit and in truth." Hollow forms of worship are but the "sacrifice of the fool," and are "abomination in his sight." The doctrine of human inability—of the utter impossibility of corrupt mortality winning the favour of a holy God, is further apparent from the consideration of the fifth petition, "Forgive us our debts as we forgive our debtors." The word rendered forgive (*aphiemen*) means literally remit. "Remit our obligations (*opheilemata*) as we remit the obligations due to us." We are under an infinite obligation to God. We owe him service, love, obedience and gratitude. We have failed to meet this obligation, and are therefore justly in the condition of the condemned debtor. Christ has assumed this debt for us, and this fifth petition is then appropriately addressed to our Surety. We ask for free remission. We pray for pardon; not upon the plea that we will incur no more debt—no creditor would accept such a plea—but we claim that the debt has been fully and perfectly paid. Poor, penniless, and dependent, we can nevertheless say to our glorious Surety, "Lord, remember us when thou comest into thy kingdom." Good works, as a ground of pardon, are as much excluded in the fifth petition as in the first. We pray that we may be forgiven, *as* (*os*) we forgive, not *because* we forgive. The fulness and freeness of our forgiveness of others is to be the *measure*, not the *cause*, of God's forgiveness of us. Just in proportion to our forbearance, toleration, and kindness towards our enemies or wrongers, will God extend his pardon and loving-kindness to us. The idea is simply this, the sinner is condemned by the *justice* of God, because of his failure to pay his debt of duty and love. Christ has interposed in *mercy* to remit that debt; but if the sinner be relentless and exacting towards those who have wronged him, then God will require him to pay "the uttermost farthing." See Matthew xviii. When we pray in the sixth petition, "Lead us not into temptation, but deliver us from evil," we of course do not charge God with being the author of sin. "Let no man say when he is tempted, I am tempted of God: for God cannot be tempted with evil, neither tempteth he any man. But every man is tempted when he is drawn away of his own lust, and enticed." James i. 13, 14. We mean to ask merely that God may keep us out of the paths of sin and temptation; that he may so dispose of our affairs, and so surround us by the restraints of his grace, that we may not incur his displeasure and wrath. We pray, like Agur, to be delivered from the elation of prosperity and the repining of adversity. We pray that all the dispensations of God's providence, and all the dealings of his hand may be sanctified to us. We pray, in short, to be guided by "the Spirit of truth," for he alone can "lead us into all truth." The petition is in its very nature addressed to the third person in the glorious Trinity, humbly beseeching his gracious influence to control the heart and life of the believer.

What a rebuke is this prayer to the empty boast of the perfectionist. God has declared the very heavens unclean in his sight, and yet a poor, polluted thing, that sprung from the dust yesterday, and will return to it to-morrow, can say that he is pure and sinless. Yea, with matchless effrontery, he can even claim not to have sinned for a score of years. He, who "knew what was in man," taught his disciples a prayer, the farthest possible removed from this self-righteous Pharisaic spirit. It breathes the language of penitence, self-distrust, and dependence. "I have sinned, forgive me my sins, and guide me for the future, that I may sin no more against thy holy name." This humble frame of mind is surely becoming a weak, fallible creature, so continually beset with temptation, and with no power in himself to resist it. There is not an event in our lives that Satan cannot make the occasion of sin. Even afflictions, which are intended to "work out a far more exceeding and eternal weight of glory," may be rendered by the adversary of souls the sources of guilt and condemnation. The plagues in Egypt but hardened the heart of Pharaoh. The afflictions of Job filled the soul of his wife with rebellion against God. The withering of his gourd made Jonah repine and wish for death. Unsanctified afflictions always harden the heart. How absurd then, the Popish doctrine, that the fires of purgatory can purify the guilty soul and fit it for heaven. Has Satan been thus purified? Have his angels been purified by the fires of the burning lake? Did the Israelites humble themselves, when they felt the pangs of thirst in the wilderness? Did not Moses call the place Meribah as well as

Massah? the place of *chiding* as well as of *temptation?* The Israelites were but types of our apostate, rebellious race. To all of us, the waters of Massah would also be the waters of Meribah, but for the sanctifying influences of his Spirit. But blessed be his holy name, light may be made to come out of darkness, and the believer be enabled to say, "it is good for me that I have been afflicted." As God set his glorious arch in the heavens, right over the wild waste of waters of the deluge, and painted it with sun-beams on the very clouds that had wrought the desolation; so he often places his bow of promise over our ruined hopes and wrecked affections, gilds it with rays from the Sun of Righteousness, and makes it more gorgeous and beautiful by the black storm-cloud of trouble in the back-ground.

There is one point that deserves our special consideration in the petition, "Lead us not into temptation." Those who use it should be careful to avoid all occasions of temptation. It is but a mockery of God to pray against temptation, and then wilfully to throw ourselves in the way of it. David may have gone upon the housetop to pray, when his roving eye prompted him to lust and murder. We are commanded to watch, as well as pray. We are too apt to neglect the former, and then call the calamities that result from our own folly and perverseness, trials of our faith, or providences of God. Thus too, many who live in open violation of all the laws of health, regard their sickness as "a chastening of the Lord."

The sickness is no doubt of the Lord, but has it not been sent because his physical laws have been broken? The assassin may as well claim immunity for the blow of his dagger, as the self-made invalid for the neglect of his health. Have we any more right to be careless of our own lives than of the lives of others?

In our translation, "Deliver us from evil," the article *the* (*tou*) has been omitted. Literally, the petition is, "Deliver us from *the* evil." The same words which are here translated "evil," are translated "the wicked one," in Matthew xiii. 19 and 38. 1 John ii. 13, iii. 12. We think that they ought to have been translated so here. There are three sources of sin—the world, the flesh, and the devil. The sixth petition pleads for deliverance from all these. Probably, "temptation" refers to the evil influence of the world, and the depraved inclinations of our own natures. We pray that we may be so guided in our intercourse with the world, and so sanctified in our desires, that we may not be "led into temptation," and then add, "deliver us" from the power, the malice and evil suggestions of the great adversary of our souls.

This view is somewhat strengthened by the fact that the word rendered "deliver," means more rigidly "break* off"—as we break off a chain. May we not have a reference to those "chains of darkness," with which Satan binds his followers, and with which he

* Adam Clarke.

himself will be eventually bound? 2 Peter ii. 4, Jude 6, Rev. xx. 3. If so, have we not expressed the compound idea of entire subjection to Satan and the progressive nature of sin? The sinner is represented in the Scriptures as the bond-servant of the great enemy of mankind. "Know ye not, that to whom ye yield yourselves servants to obey, his servants ye are to whom ye obey; whether of sin unto death, or of obedience unto righteousness?" Rom. vi. 16. "Whosoever committeth sin, is the servant of sin." John viii. 34. "While they promise themselves liberty, they themselves are the servants of corruption; *for of whom a man is overcome, of the same is he brought in bondage.*" 2 Peter ii. 19. Was not the bondage in Egypt but a type of the more cruel subjection to sin and Satan?

Sin is progressive. As the chain which the adversary of souls throws around his victims is composed of links, so sin follows sin in a regular concatenated series. The Roman tyrant, whose atrocities have been the wonder of the world for so many generations, began his career of cruelty with the torture of flies. "What, is thy servant a dog that he should do this great thing," replied the indignant Syrian leader, when told by the prophet Elisha the enormities that he should commit. And yet he advanced step by step in his career of crime, until he had committed all the horrible cruelties that were predicted. So, too, with David, the wanton look was followed by lust, adultery, deception, and murder.

We cannot conclude our notice of the Lord's Prayer without making the obvious remark, that the great object of desire in it is the glory of the triune God. "The Lord has made all things for himself, even the sinner for the day of evil." We are bound then to "glorify him with our bodies and our spirits, which are his." The prayer taught by our Saviour embodies this central idea. It begins with invocation and ends with praise. God is first and God is last in it. The one special petition is "Hallowed be thy name"—and that it may be hallowed, we pray for the coming of Christ's kingdom, and the fulfilment of his holy will on earth as it is in heaven. Even our personal petitions have reference to the same thing. We ask that we may be fed "with food convenient for us, lest we be poor and steal, and take the name of our God in vain." Prov. xxx. 8, 9. We ask for the pardon of our sins, so that no longer oppressed with the sense of guilt, "a new song may be put in our mouths, even praise unto our God." Ps. xl. 3. We ask that the Holy Spirit may lead us out of the paths of temptation, and deliver us from the bondage of Satan, in order "that we may show forth the praises of him who hath called us out of darkness into his marvellous light." 1 Peter ii. 9. The supply of our temporal wants, the pardon of our sins, and the sanctification of our natures, are all sought as means to one great end—that "the King, eternal, invisible, the only wise God, may have honour and glory for ever, Amen." 1 Tim. i. 17.

It is a remarkable and a most significant fact, that our Saviour only commented on that portion of the Lord's Prayer which relates to the forgiveness of injuries. "For if ye forgive men their trespasses, your Heavenly Father will also forgive you. But if ye forgive not men their trespasses, neither will your Father forgive your trespasses." (Verses 14, 15.) The reason of this special comment is plain. Jesus knew the heart of man. "All things are naked and opened unto the eyes of him with whom we have to do." Heb. iv. 3. He knew that the hardest duty, even for the Christian, is the duty of forgiveness. Luke tells us that, when on a certain occasion our Saviour had reiterated the command to forgive, the Apostles cried out, "Lord increase our faith." They felt their inability to accord obedience, without a larger supply of grace. Revenge was a virtue among the cultivated Greeks and Romans. The wisest and best of their philosophers inculcated it as a duty. The refined Athenians built temples and erected altars to Até, the goddess of hatred and vengeance. The American Indian thinks that the Great Spirit will be offended with him, if he permit personal and family wrongs to go unavenged. Nearly all the wars that have desolated our earth and drenched it with blood, have been prompted by the fell spirit of vengeance. Was it not the infernal thirst of Satan for revenge, that brought death and sin into the world?—that changed the bloom and fragrance of Paradise into thorns and thistles, rottenness and putridity?—that changed the hymn of praise and song of gratitude into horrid blasphemy and the wail of despair? The spirit of revenge is the spirit of the pit of darkness. It should find no resting-place in the bosom of a child of God and an heir of the skies. Even according to heathen mythology, Ate was thrust out from heaven. If a heathen Jupiter, with all his abominations, could not tolerate so foul a spirit, how can we expect *our* Heavenly Father to look upon it with the least allowance? He has forbidden revenge in the most solemn manner. The Jew was not even allowed to hate his oppressor, the Egyptian. While the Israelite was yet smarting under a sense of his wrongs in Egypt, God proclaimed by the mouth of Moses, "thou shalt not abhor an Egyptian." Deut. xxiii. 7. There are many other positive prohibitions against revenge in the books of Moses. See particularly, Exod. xxiii. 4, 5, and Levit. xix. 18. The Apostle Paul, following up the teaching of Moses and our Saviour, has forbidden us from requiting our own wrongs, upon the highest possible ground. "Avenge not yourselves, but rather give place unto wrath: for it is written, Vengeance is mine, I will repay, saith the Lord." Rom. xii. 19. He who takes the redress of his injuries in his own hands, is thus shown to arrogate to himself a right belonging exclusively to God. "Shall not the Judge of all the earth do right?" May we not leave the rectification of all our wrongs in his hands?

There are several things in the 14th and 15th verses above quoted, which deserve our particular attention. The substitution of trespasses for debts, (*paraptomata* for *opheilemata*,) is peculiarly significant. The word rendered "trespasses," comes from a verb that means "to fall off." Trespasses are then "fallings off," failings, little slips in duty. If ye forgive men their little failings, your Heavenly Father will forgive *you*, not your little failings, but you, the great debtor. If you will forgive your fellow-servant the hundred pence due you, your Master will pardon you for the ten thousand talents due to him. Matt. xviii. But if ye forgive not men their little failings, neither will your Father forgive you your little failings. He will hold you to account, even to the uttermost farthing. The non-repetition of trespasses in the 14th verse, and its repetition in the 15th, are peculiarly instructive. The omission shows that the pardon, extended to the kind and forgiving, embraces both their great sins and little failings, (both *opheilemata* and *paraptomata;*) while the repetition shows that the relentless and unforgiving are held to a strict account for small as well as great offences. Again, the omission of the adjective "heavenly," in the 15th verse, is full of meaning. God is the Father of the wicked and unforgiving, as well as of the holy and gentle, but he is not their "heavenly" Father. Heaven is his holy habitation. The revengeful can never meet him there. They cannot speak of him, as absent children speak of a beloved parent away at the old homestead, where they one day expect to join him.

The importance of a full, hearty, and perfect forgiveness of our enemies, cannot be over-estimated. Christ has made it the test of discipleship. The Father has declined being called heavenly Parent by the revengeful and unforgiving. They have nothing heavenly about them. Heaven is peopled by the forgiven and the forgiving. We are in a fearful condition, if we are deluding ourselves as to the reality of our free forgiveness. If the monster revenge have been lurking in our bosoms, and we all unconscious of his presence, is there no spear of Ithuriel to dissolve the enchantment and show him in all his hideous proportions? May we not apply this test to the sincerity of our professions of forgiveness? Would we rather hear good than evil spoken of our enemy? Do we rejoice in his *lawful* prosperity? Do we take sincere delight in praying for him? If we are gratified by the good fame of our enemy, when fully deserved; by his success in life, honestly gained; and if, in addition, we can feel it to be a privilege to pray for him, we may safely conclude that we have no malice against him in our hearts. But we are not bound to rejoice in the ill-deserved reputation of our enemy, nor in his dishonest gains. Still, if his unlawful success give us pain, not because it is *unlawful*, but because it is *success*, we may be sure that he is not forgiven.

FASTING.

"Moreover, when ye fast, be not as the hypocrites, of a sad countenance: for they disfigure their faces that they may appear unto men to fast. Verily, I say unto you, they have their reward. But thou, when thou fastest, anoint thy head and wash thy face; that thou appear not unto men to fast, but unto thy Father which is in secret: and thy Father, which seeth in secret, shall reward thee openly." (Verses 16–18.) Our Saviour, in these verses, prescribes the rules which are to regulate his disciples in that important religious duty, fasting. We notice that the language of our Saviour implies the observance of fasting on the part of his disciples—"*When* ye fast." It would indeed be strange, if Christians neglected a duty, whose binding obligation has been felt by the Jews, by the Mohammedans, and even by the heathen, from the remotest time to the present day. Brown of Haddington, well observes, "The light of nature and word of God direct us, that whenever we have fallen into grievous sins; when we feel or fear the infliction of God's judgments; or when we have distinguished need of some special mercy and assistance, we ought, by fasting and prayer, solemnly to bewail our sins, supplicate forgiveness thereof, implore the averting or removal of judgments, and request the bestowal of necessary favour and help." So clearly has the light of nature (as above stated) made fasting a duty, that there probably never existed a nation which did not observe stated fasts. The Jews had an annual fast on the 10th day of the month Tisri. The Egyptians, Phœnicians, Assyrians, Greeks, and Romans, had also their stated fasts. The Roman Emperors were accustomed to observe these days with great solemnity. We read of the fasting of Numa Pompilius, Julius Cæsar, Augustus, Vespasian, and others. Mahomet enjoined this duty in an especial manner upon all his followers. He was accustomed to say that "fasting was the gate of heaven, and that the odour of the mouth of him who fasteth is more grateful to God than that of musk." Pythagoras and all his sect rigidly performed the duty of fasting. The North American Indians were accustomed to set apart days for fasting before engaging in war. Fasting is an important religious exercise among the Hindoos, the Tartars, the Chinese, &c., who live at the present day. Two ideas seem to have pervaded the human mind universally. The first is, that "without shedding of blood, there can be no remission of sin." For bloody sacrifices have existed everywhere, in all ages of the world. The second is, that offended Deity may be appeased by fasting, humiliation, and prayer. These two ideas are more universal even than the tradition of the deluge.

The Holy Scriptures record many instances of fasting, and of God's gracious acceptance of some of them. Moses fasted thrice for the space of forty days. Elijah and our Saviour, each once for the same period. David fasted during the sickness of his child. Part of the threatened calamity was averted from Ahab, because of his humiliation and fasting. Daniel was fasting when the angel Gabriel was caused to fly swiftly with a gracious answer to his prayer. The fast and repentance of the Ninevites saved them from destruction. The mourning, fasting, and prayer of Esther, Mordecai, and their people, thwarted the wicked schemes of Haman, and preserved the Jewish nation from destruction. Jehoshaphat and his subjects observed a solemn fast when they heard of the invasion of the Moabites and Edomites; and the Lord gave his people a miraculous victory over their enemies. 2 Chron. xx.

The universal recognition of fasting as a religious duty, the example of our Saviour, and the holy men of old, the gracious acceptance of God—all these teach us that fasting is a very important part of devotion. The neglect of this great duty in Protestant countries, may be owing somewhat to the contempt felt for the mock fasts of the Romish Church. It becomes us, however, to reflect that our aversion for Popish festivals, and Popish rites and ceremonies, can never excuse us for the non-observance of a high and sacred duty. The fact that our Saviour did not prescribe the time, the length, and the occasion of fasts, does not prove that he did not regard abstinence from food, at special seasons, as a religious exercise. It only proves that his religion is not one of ritualism and formalism. Had he given particular rules in regard to these things, a solemn devotional service would have been converted into an empty form—like the Lent of the Romish Church. Men are prone to make their religion consist in forms and ceremonies. God requires spiritual worship. Christ enjoined on his disciples the inner worship of the heart, and not the outer of unmeaning rites. This accounts for his not giving any directions about the proper posture in prayer, nor in regard to the mode of baptism, &c. Bigotry and formalism attach great importance to externals, our Saviour attached none. The inference then is rash, that because he did not leave minute instructions to regulate fasting, therefore it is not a duty. The same reasoning would apply, with as much force, to baptism, alms-giving, and prayer. The example of our Saviour, and his language, when speaking of fasting, are sufficient to show how he regarded it. He has wisely left the performance of the duty to be modified by the age, the health, and the condition of the penitent.

It may be well to notice critically, a few of the words employed in the preceding verses. The word rendered "fast" is a compound, and means literally "not to eat." This signification is sufficient to explode the theory of some, that fasting is abstinence from sin and not from food. Isaiah has taught us that during the season of fast, we should endeavour to remember the wrongs that we have committed, and make ample redress to the injured; but he does not tell us that we are not to abstain from food. He merely corrects a too common error with formalists, that the outward act is acceptable to God.

The word rendered "hypocrites," means more literally, dissemblers, stage-actors. The godless are prone to charge Christians with hypocrisy, and infidels have had the effrontery to denounce the religion of our blessed Redeemer on this very ground. Now there would be something fair and manly in this denunciation of scepticism, if our Saviour had encouraged hypocrisy, or had even failed to censure it. But where can there be found more solemn rebukes of this grievous sin, than in the public instructions of our Lord? Were there ever more fearful woes uttered than those he pronounced against the hypocritical Scribes and Pharisees? See Matt. xxiii. And does he not teach in this very Sermon on the Mount, that God "seeth in secret"—that he cannot be deceived, and will not be mocked? Our Saviour will not claim a hypocrite as his disciple; what right then has the scoffer to place him in the ranks of the Redeemer?

The word rendered "sad," might have been more appropriately translated "sour," or "morose." The hypocrite may well be "morose." God abhors him, the world despises him, and conscience troubles him. In the whole universe there is no more pitiable, and no less pitied creature than he.

The rebuke of moroseness, contained in the above verses, should be well pondered by every Christian. Surely he, of all men on earth, ought to be cheerful. How can he who has God for his friend, and heaven for his home, indulge in sullenness and gloom? Come what may, he knows that "it shall be well with the righteous." He may lose children, friends, health, reputation, property, still he knows that "all things shall work together for his good." Let him then show forth his cheerfulness and "contentment," as well as his "godliness," that others may get "great gain" from his example. The moroseness and austerity of some professed Christians, have done much injury to the cause of the Redeemer, and brought great reproach upon his religion. The sour countenance of Pharisaic disciples have often made the young regard Christianity as the embodiment of all that is dismal and lugubrious; and thus a stone of stumbling has been thrown in the way of the youthful and light-hearted. Historians tell us that the ribaldry, buffoonery, and gross licentiousness, during the reign of Charles II. of England, were brought about in good part, by the national disgust at the cant, nasal tones, long prayers, and sour visages, of the Puritans. Those who could not appreciate the bright and noble qualities of the Puritans, could ridicule their dress and manner. Had the purest and best men, that the world has ever produced, been more cheerful, more joyous, more courteous, and more conciliating, England might have been spared the ignominy of the disgraceful reigns of Charles II. and James II. The fact is, that the Puritans at the outset never could have gained a party sufficiently strong to overthrow the throne of Charles I., but for the popularity of their great leader, John Hampden. All know how much of this popularity was due to that "natural cheerfulness, vivacity, and flowing courtesy to all men," of which Clarendon speaks. The broad and genial humour of John Bunyan, makes him more read than any other author. The same quality in Spurgeon makes him the most popular of living preachers. Our Saviour, though "a man of sorrow, and acquainted with grief," yet mixed freely with the people in kind and cheerful conversation. He honoured a marriage by his presence. He ate with publicans and sinners. He talked with a poor ignorant woman by the well of Samaria. He wept with the bereaved sisters at the grave of their brother Lazarus. All this shows a disposition the farthest removed from the sullen and selfish gloom of morbid religion.

COVETOUSNESS.

"Lay not up for yourselves treasures upon earth, where moth and rust doth corrupt, and where thieves break through and steal: but lay up for yourselves treasures in heaven, where neither moth nor rust doth corrupt, and where thieves do not break through nor steal: for where your treasure is, there will your heart be also." (Verses 19—21.)

The last verse explains the meaning of the word "treasure," as employed here, and also points out the connection between these three verses and those which immediately precede them. Treasure is any thing upon which the heart is set; whether that be wealth, rank, reputation, worldly grandeur, friends, luxury, or what not. The Pharisees made the good opinion of men their treasure, and were ostentatious in alms-giving, prayer, and fasting, to gain that good opinion. Our Saviour, after condemning them for seeking this species of treasure, proceeds to warn his disciples against every other form of worldliness. Special reference may be had to the inordinate thirst for wealth —the low sordid vice of covetousness. This is the great sin of the Church—the great sin of the age—the sin that dishonours God and brings reproach upon the Christian name—the sin that "tramples under foot the blood of the covenant, and esteems it an unholy thing." Twenty-five hundred years ago, the Prophet Amos lifted up his warning voice against the low, debasing vice, that hardens all within, and stifles every generous emotion and kindly sympathy. The covetous "sells the righteous for silver, and the poor for a pair of shoes, and pants after the dust of the earth on the head of the poor." Amos ii. 6, 7. The covetous takes away all that the poor working man has, and then begrudges him the little dust that the sweat of labour has accumulated on his brow! The Saviour took up the warning, and taught, "Lay not up for yourselves treasure upon earth." But spite of his teaching, the broad road to death is thronged with the followers of Mammon; hell is overflowing with his worshippers. The great Apostle to the Gentiles, who had studied so much, travelled so much, and gained such an intimate acquaintance with human nature, has left his testimony that "covetousness is idolatry," and that "they who will be rich, fall into temptation and a snare, and into many foolish and hurtful lusts, which drown men in destruction and perdition. For, the love of money is the root of all evil: which, while some coveted after, they have erred from the faith, and pierced themselves through with many sorrows." Col. iii. 5; 1 Tim. vi. 9, 10. All history, and all experience confirm the testimony, that the covetous *do* fall into many foolish and hurtful lusts, and *do* pierce themselves through with many sorrows. But is the world any wiser and better from the instruction of the "Philosophy that teaches by example"? Were mankind ever so absorbed, body and soul, in the pursuit of wealth, as in the middle of this the nineteenth century? How many of the votaries of Mammon would almost as soon think of giving their hearts' blood, as any portion of their wealth, to advance the kingdom of their Redeemer. Alas, the mighty dollar looms up before them with a lustre and brilliance sufficient to obscure the beams of the Sun of Righteousness.

The disciple, who had the distinction of being the first Bishop of Jerusalem, who was the near relative, if not the brother, of our Lord, and who was the only one of the disciples honoured by a private interview with the risen Saviour, (1 Cor. xv. 7,) denounces covetousness in the strongest terms. "Your gold and silver is cankered; and the rust of them shall be a witness against you, and shall eat your flesh as it were fire. Ye have heaped treasure together for the last days." James v. 3. There is no mistaking this language. Riches, which are allowed to *rust*, because not employed in the service of Christ, shall be converted into penal fires in the great day of

Judgment, and shall burn and torture their wretched possessors for ever and for ever.

When the great Jewish law-giver came into the presence of the worshippers of the golden calf, he threw down and broke into pieces the tables of the law written by the finger of God himself. Here we have taught in a symbol, the melancholy fact, of perpetual recurrence, though we as perpetually shut our eyes against it, that God's holy law is ever thrown down and trampled under foot, when gold is set up as an object of idolatry. Our court-houses, our jails, our penitentiaries, our gibbets, proclaim the same truth. The wail comes up from the lurid flames of perdition, "we despised and trampled upon the commandments of the Most High, from the cursed thirst for gold, *and we are here.*" Moreover, the story of the broken tables of the law, teaches us the brutish nature of the worship of Mammon. "We are sick," says the eloquent Macaulay, "like the children of Israel, of the objects of our old and legitimate worship. We pine for a new idolatry. All that is costly and all that is ornamental in our intellectual treasures must be delivered up and cast into the furnace," that there may come out a calf for rational and immortal creatures to fall down and worship. God is a Spirit, and his service is spiritual and elevating; the worship of Mammon, like that of the golden calf, is brutalizing and degrading. But while covetousness is a base and brutish sin in the man of the world, it is a crime of the blackest dye in the professed Christian.

God cannot be deceived, he will not be mocked. With what abhorrence must he listen to the prayer of the nominal Christian, "Thy kingdom come, thy will be done," when, at the same time that he prays, he grasps his purse-strings with the tenacity of death, and gives nothing, or the merest trifle, to advance the interests of that kingdom, and promote compliance with that holy will. There is an awful mockery in the prayer that might make Satan and his infernal hosts shudder with horror. Talk to this mocker about the claims of the Church of Christ upon his substance, and he is as deaf, and cold, and inanimate as the granite blocks of New Hampshire. But the slightest whisper of gain, will vibrate upon his auditory nerve with a thrill that is felt in his inmost soul.

Our Saviour has given us the best of all reasons for indifference to worldly treasures—their insecurity. "The fashion of this world passeth away." Passing away, is written upon all beneath the skies. "Riches certainly make themselves wings; they fly away, as an eagle toward heaven." Fame is the breath of the fickle multitude, who cry hosannah one day, and crucify him the next. Relations and friends will die. The worm will feast and batten on those we love as our own souls.

> "The knell, the shroud, the mattock, and the grave,
> The deep damp vault, the darkness, and the worm."

O, with what appalling emphasis they proclaim the folly of setting our affections upon anything earthly. The Lord alone "changes not." Mal. iii. 6. Father in Heaven, help us to love thee supremely, so that we may have an enduring treasure left, when the vines that cluster in beauty and fragrance around our heads, wither like Jonah's gourd from the gnawing of the worm at the root.

Critical exegesis. The word rendered "moth" comes from a verb, which signifies to putrefy. The word rendered "rust" is from a verb that means to eat. "Thieves break through" might have been more literally rendered, "thieves *dig* through." The houses in the East are generally made of sun-dried brick, and the walls can readily be dug through. The houses in Mexico are chiefly of the *adobes*, and in the attack on Monterey the American troops advanced into the heart of the city by digging occasionally through the walls of courts and houses. They thus kept themselves sheltered from the view and fire of the enemy.

We are taught impressively by the allusions to the moth, the rust, and the thieves, the uncertainty of earthly possessions, whether they consist in dress, money, or dwellings. The animal and the mineral kingdom are at war against our treasures. Even our fellow-creatures seek to rob and despoil us of them. Why then should we set our hearts upon a thing so uncertain as worldly wealth? Let us learn to lay up our store in "heaven." This word is in the singular number in the original, and means the local habitation of glorified spirits. There only, is there security. Even a heathen philosopher could perceive the folly of boasting about uncertain riches. Herodotus tells us that when Crœsus, king of Lydia, boastfully exhibited his vast treasures to Solon, the Athenian philosopher, and inquired of him if he would not pronounce the owner thereof the happiest of men; Solon plainly told him that he could call no man happy before his death, because it could not be foreseen what would happen unto him. This same Crœsus was in fact besieged in Sardis, by Cyrus the Mede, and on the capture of the city, was condemned to be burned to death. When the soldiers were piling the faggots around the unhappy Crœsus, he cried aloud three times, "Solon, Solon, Solon." This so excited the curiosity of Cyrus that he inquired the reason of the exclamation, and upon being told of what Solon had said, he began to reflect upon the precariousness of his own power and the insecurity of his own treasures, and was so softened by the reflection, that he pardoned Crœsus, and ever after treated him with kindness. If the testimony of Herodotus, Diodorus Siculus, and Justin, can be relied upon, Cyrus may well have felt the uncertainty of his own position, for they say that he perished in battle with the Scythians.

CONSCIENCE.

"The light of the body is the eye: if therefore thine eye be single, thy whole body shall be full of light. But if thine eye be evil, thy whole body shall be full of darkness. If therefore the light that is in thee be darkness, how great is that darkness!" (Verses 22, 23.)

These verses explain the nature and office of conscience. Two things are necessary to clearness of vision—sufficiency of light and soundness of eye. Two things are indispensable, in order that the *dicta* of conscience may be infallible—an enlightened understanding and a sanctified heart. The former is represented in the beautiful figure of our Saviour, by light—the usual symbol of knowledge. The latter is symbolized by the eye; for the eye guides and directs the natural man, as the heart does the moral man. "Out of the heart are the issues of life." "Out of the abundance of the heart, the mouth speaketh." Our moral movements are thus shown to be controlled by the heart, just as our natural movements are by the eye. If the eye be perfectly healthy and abundantly supplied with light, its perception will be unerring within the limit of vision. So if the understanding be perfectly enlightened, and the heart be perfectly sanctified, conscience will always approve the right and disapprove the wrong. But conscience is a very unsafe guide, unless these two conditions be perfectly fulfilled. Its monitions were unerring before the fall. They have never been so since. And just in proportion to the ignorance and corruption of man does the voice of conscience "give an uncertain sound." Just here lies the mistake of fanaticism. The fanatic places his conscience above the Bible, yea, above God himself. He makes conscience a rule of right—a guide in moral conduct. It is no such thing. It is simply a faculty of mind, which approves our conduct when *consistent* with our ideas of right, and disapproves our conduct when *inconsistent* with those ideas. This is conscience in its perfect state; but it may be "seared as with a hot iron," (1 Tim. iv. 2,) and neither approve nor disapprove. "The word of God, which is contained in the Scriptures of the Old and New Testaments, is the only rule to direct us how we may glorify and enjoy him." Persecuting Saul, when "he verily thought within himself that he ought to do many things contrary to the name of Jesus of Nazareth," had just as approving a conscience as the martyr Paul at the tribunal of Nero. The Ammonite mother, when she placed her child in the arms of the thrice-heated image of Moloch, had just as much the approbation of her conscience, as had the pious Hannah when she devoted her unborn child to the service of the living God. The approving conscience sustains the Hindoo widow when she mounts the funeral pile of her husband, to be burnt to ashes. The fact is that men *cannot* embark in any enterprise with the clamour of conscience against them. They must either stifle it or win it to their side. "Conscience makes cowards of us all," said the greatest of uninspired men. This accounts for the extraordinary ingenuity of all mankind in framing excuses and making palliations for their conduct. Adam laid his sin at the door of Eve, and she excused herself and criminated the serpent. Thus it has ever been with all their descendants. "All the ways of a man are right in his own eyes," said the wise king of Israel. We are inclined to think that few have the hardihood knowingly and wilfully to commit an act that they believe at the time to be heinously sinful. From what the Bible teaches us of the temptations of Satan, we learn that the art of the great Adversary consists in making sin appear venial or altogether innocent. Thus he tempted our Saviour to cast himself from the pinnacle of the temple, that he might cause a prophecy concerning the Messiah to be fulfilled. The most cruel and remorseless of persecutors have ever been those whose consciences approved of their persecution.

Catherine de Medicis could go in solemn procession to return thanks to the Most High, for the massacre of St. Bartholomew. Laud was the most unfeeling of persecutors, because the most conscientious of bigots. Cotton Mather was zealous in the cause of religion when busiest in torturing old women for witchcraft. Again, we have another phase of perverted conscience in the impure and licentious. "Unto the pure all things are pure: but unto them that are defiled and unbelieving is nothing pure; but even their mind and conscience is defiled." Tit. i. 15. Adultery, fornication, and polygamy, have had their advocates and defenders. Infidels of learning and intelligence have contended that there was nothing wrong in these things. Again, we have another phase of perverted conscience in the hypocrite, whose whole life is a lie, yet who so sears his conscience that its monitions give him no trouble. "Speaking lies in hypocrisy; having their consciences seared with a hot iron." 1 Tim. iv. 2. Again, we have another phase of perverted conscience in the turbulent, the litigious, and the brawling, who justifies his evil passions, and exclaims with Jonah, "I do well to be angry, even unto death." And so the murderer, the duellist, the rake, the robber; each has his plea of justification of his crimes. No one understood the tricks of conscience better than the Apostle Paul, who had himself been the dupe of it. We find him accordingly speaking of a "defiled conscience," Titus i. 15; of a "seared conscience;" of an "evil conscience," Heb. x. 22: again, of a "conscience purged from dead works," Heb. ix. 14; of a "pure conscience," 1 Tim. iii. 9; of a "good conscience," Heb. xiii. 18; of a "conscience void of offence toward God and toward men." Acts xxiv. 16. If Paley had studied the teachings of God's word in regard to conscience, he never could have said, "It seems to me either that there exists no such instincts as compose what is callod tho moral sense, or that they are not now to be distinguished from prejudices and habits." He had observed that these instincts depended upon "the exigencies, the climate, situation, or local circumstances of the country," and, therefore, he justly concluded, that all this "looked very little like the steady hand and indelible characters of nature." The blunder of Paley and all of his school is easily exposed. They mistook entirely the nature and office of conscience. Believing it to be the function of conscience to give infallible directions in regard to moral deportment, and perceiving that men in every age of the world had committed the most atrocious crimes, conscientiously and in good faith, they concluded that there was no such thing as the moral sense. Their reasoning is sound, but their premise is wrong. Conscience is not a moral guide. The word of God is our only rule of right. It alone is "a lamp to our feet, and a light to our path." Conscience is a safe pilot over the turbid sea of life to him alone whose mind is perfectly wise, and whose heart is perfectly pure. Just as the eye points out the right path, when it has plenty of light, and there is no visual defect. All sin proceeds either from ignorance or innate depravity, or from both combined. The heathen and the uncultivated may wish to serve God aright, but they have not the requisite knowledge. Light is wanting. The refined and educated sinner hates God, because his heart is wicked. The eye itself is unsound. "O send out thy light and thy truth," was the prayer of David, and should be the prayer of every child of God. The last command of the risen Saviour, before leaving this scene of his suffering, was to spread abroad this light and this truth. One-half of what is spent in luxury and folly by those who profess to obey the Lord Jesus, would place a copy of the Holy Scriptures in the hands of every living creature. But even should this great and glorious work be accomplished, there would yet remain much to be done. Light is not all that is needed. Knowledge, even religious knowledge, cannot save the soul. The doctors of the Sorbonne, the learned cardinals of the consistories of Rome, may know the truth and hate it too. To cultivate the intellect and leave the heart unaffected, is but to increase the capacity for evil. The learning of Germany has run into pantheistic infidelity. The splendid achievements of France in literature and the arts and sciences, are only surpassed by her heaven-defying wickedness. The traveller Livingstone tells us, that the most corrupt portions of Africa are those which have been in contact with European intelligence and civilization.

We ought not then merely to send out the light of God's word to "the dark places of the earth, which are full of the habitations of cruelty," but we ought also earnestly to pray that his Holy Spirit may carry home the truth to the heart and conscience of the whole heathen world.

We cannot dismiss the subject of conscience without referring to its fearful stings in the world of endless woe. We have seen that ignorance and the depravity of the heart modify the effects of conscience in this life. The corruption of our natures has a twofold influence. It makes us listen to the suggestions of evil passions, and also to the temptations of Satan. But these three modifying influences do not exist in hell. Knowledge is perfect there. The sinner there perceives the enormity of his crimes in the light of eternity. He then understands perfectly the amazing folly and wickedness of rejecting a crucified Saviour. Neither will the second influence pervert conscience. There will then be no lusts to gratify. And lastly, *Satan will be on the side of conscience*, to add to the torture of the poor lost soul. His taunts and jeers will echo back the merciless rebukes of conscience. Penitence will then be changed into remorse, and conscience into the worm that never dies.

> "With a thousand snaky heads
> Eyed each with double orbs of glaring wrath;
> And with as many tails, that twisted out
> In horrid revolution, tipped with stings;
> And all its mouths, that wide and darkly gaped,
> And breathed most poisonous breath, had each a sting
> Forked, and long, and venomous, and sharp;
> And, in its writhings infinite, it grasped
> Malignantly what seemed a heart, swollen, black,
> And quivering with torture most intense;
> And still the heart, with anguish throbbing high,
> Made effort to escape, but could not; for
> Howe'er it turned, and oft it vainly turned,
> These complicated foldings held it fast.
> And still the monstrous beast with sting of head
> Or tail transpierced it, bleeding evermore."*

None can think this picture too highly coloured, who have observed the torture inflicted by awakened conscience even in this world, where all are ready "with some sweet oblivious antidote to cleanse the

* Course of Time, Book I.

foul bosom of that perilous stuff which weighs upon the heart." How often do we hear of men preferring the agonies of death to the stings of remorse, and of their risking the terrors of eternity, rather than endure the agony of conscious guilt. Thus Judas hanged himself, rather than bear the reproaches of conscience. The days, and especially the nights, of Charles IX. of France, after the massacre of St. Bartholomew, are described as having been full of horror and agony unutterable. His murdered victims seemed ever to be stalking into his presence, "shaking their gory locks at him." His mental suffering was so great, at times, that the blood burst through the pores of his skin. Hear the language of one, whose worst sins were scarce so black as the best virtues of Charles. "I walked," says John Bunyan, "to a neighbouring town, and sat down on a settle in the street, and fell into a very deep muse about the most fearful state my sins had brought me to; but methought I saw as if the sun that shineth in the heavens did grudge to give me light; and as if the very stones in the streets and tiles upon the houses did band themselves against me. Methought that they all combined together to banish me out of the world. I was abhorred of them and unfit to dwell among them, because I had sinned against the Saviour. O, how happy now was every creature over I, for they stood fast and kept their station; but I was gone and lost." If conscience can produce such horrible effects in this world, where ignorance, pride, self-love, and the delusions of Satan, all conspire to blunt its sting, how fearful must be its torture amid the sulphureous waves of perdition. The dreadfulness of that torment, eye hath not seen, nor ear heard, neither hath it entered into the heart of man. Memory is imperfect now, and can only goad for one sin out of a thousand. But memory will be perfect in that world of woe, and will make every sin pass in review before the lost soul, as the great English dramatist feigns that the ghosts of his murdered victims were marshalled before the fiendish Richard on Bosworth Field.

There is a peculiar significance in the employment of light, as the symbol of knowledge. Light proceeds from the sun. So all knowledge, all truth, must come from "God manifest in the flesh," Jesus Christ, the Sun of Righteousness. Before our world was irradiated by his beams, how dark, confused, and chaotic was even the wisdom of the heathen philosophers. The learned Athenians mocked, when Paul talked about the resurrection of the dead. The doctrine of the immortality of the soul, of a future state of rewards and punishments, of one self-existent, eternal, invisible God, was rejected by the greatest poets, statesmen, legislators, and sages of antiquity. Their religion consisted in the worship of brutes, and of beings who were but the personifications of every species of wickedness. The wise Egyptians and the refined Assyrians worshipped the bull. The Jupiter and Juno, Mars and Venus, &c., of Rome and Greece, in the most cultivated period of their history, were monsters of depravity. Mount Olympus, the residence of the gods, was the scene of anger, strife, jealousy, intrigue, and licentiousness. The purest of the heathen philosophers had no conception of a heaven of holiness. Jesus Christ brought life and immortality to light. His gospel alone contains a pure system of morality. It alone gives just and exalted views of the "King, immortal, invisible, the only wise God." And here we may remark, that the sages of antiquity erred in regard to the nature of light itself. Their most eminent mathematicians regarded it as an emanation from the eye itself, and not from the great luminary of day. Their theory is exactly parallel with that of the infidel perfectionists of our day, who contend that weak, sinful man has power in himself, without aid from above, to gain all wisdom, all knowledge, all holiness. Is not this view condemned by the very figure employed in the Scriptures to convey the idea of knowledge and virtue? As light must come from the source of light, so must all wisdom descend from above. The attainments of mankind, without the aid of the Bible, bear the same relation to true knowledge, that the light of the feeble lamp made by human hands bears to the full blaze of the meridian sun, set up in the heavens by God himself.

"If thine eye be single," &c. The word rendered *single*, conveys the idea of that which is simple, not complex, not distorted, not looking in two directions. It may probably be best explained by reference to the properties of luminous matter. Light is rectilinear, its line of direction is straight. If the eye then look directly forward, a true image will be painted on the retina, and the man will see clearly the object gazed at. But if the eye be rolling from earth to heaven, trying to take in the glories of both, a false, distorted image will be pictured, and nothing will be seen distinctly. This explains the connection between these two verses and the preceding. The Pharisees gave alms, fasted, and prayed, to glorify God and win the favour of man. They had the rolling eye, and everything appeared distorted and in unnatural proportions. They had light enough, abundance of religious knowledge, but the eye itself was unsound, and "the whole body was full of darkness." In truth, when the eye is unsound, an excess of light but increases the indistinctness of vision. The diseased organ cannot endure the glare. "Not many wise are called," said the Apostle Paul. What are known as *diffraction bands* in optics, present luminous spots for a certain amount of light, but if that amount be increased, all is darkness. Just so it is in spiritual matters. An increase of knowledge, whether literary, scientific, or religious, that is not received into a sound and healthy heart, will but add to the darkness and folly of the blinded sinner. "The wisdom of this world is foolishness with God." "The natural man receiveth not the things which are of the Spirit of God."

The unbelief of the wise and learned often puzzles weak believers. They forget the teachings of our

Saviour. They forget that soundness of eye, as well as sufficiency of light, are necessary to clearness of vision. They forget that the poor Pharisee missed seeing the glories of heaven, because he attempted to gaze, at the same time, at the loveliness of earth.

DOUBLE SERVICE.

"No man can serve two masters: for either he will hate the one, and love the other; or else he will hold to the one, and despise the other. Ye cannot serve God and Mammon." (Verse 24.)

This verse contains the third reason against indulging in worldly-mindedness. The first, founded on the insecurity of all worldly possessions, is contained in the three verses beginning at the 19th and ending with the 21st. The uncertain, perishable nature of everything earthly, is there most strikingly set forth. The folly of setting our hearts upon such transitory things, is thus most clearly shown:

"All, all on earth is shadow, all beyond
Is substance, the reverse is Folly's creed.
How solid all, where change shall be no more.
The spider's most attenuated thread
Is cord, is cable, to man's tender tie
On earthly bliss: it breaks at every breeze."

In the 22d and 23d verses, we have the second reason—covetousness perverts the conscience. It "puts darkness for light and light for darkness." It quenches the light that God has given, and "kindles a fire of its own, that men may encompass themselves about with sparks, and walk in the light of their fire and of the sparks that they have kindled." The forum, the streets, and the palaces of Rome were lighted up by the torches and flambeaux of the midnight procession to celebrate the impure rites of Cybele. And just as the light was prostituted to an unholy purpose, so is the lofty aspiration after God and holiness perverted by covetousness into the mere sordid desire for the perishing things of this world.

The third reason is given in this 24th verse, and depends upon the incompatibility of the services of God and Mammon. The word *mammon* was used in the Syrian and Punic languages to signify riches and worldly gain of whatever kind. (*Clarke.*) We understand by it in this place, *Satan tempting with the proffer of worldly wealth and worldly distinction.* On three distinct occasions, our Saviour called Satan "the Prince of this world." John xii. 31; xiv. 30; xvi. 11. St. Paul calls him "the Prince of the power of the air." Ephes. ii. 2. And we think that the remarkable language of the Apostle, in 2 Cor. iv. 4, explains fully the meaning of Mammon. "In whom the God of this world has blinded the minds of them which believe not, lest the light of the glorious gospel of Christ, who is the image of God, should shine unto them." Here the same qualities are attributed to Satan that are ascribed to Mammon, in the 23d and 24th verses under consideration. He is the god of this world, he blinds the mind, he perverts the conscience, and he is in active hostility with the Son of

God; so that no man can serve both. Assuming then that Mammon is but another name for Satan in his capacity of tempter, the meaning of the 24th verse is obvious. A subject cannot serve two sovereigns, whose wishes, commands, and interests are entirely opposite. A servant cannot love two masters, whose characters, disposition, tones of thought, and habits of life are irreconcilably different. It is impossible for a soldier to range himself, at the same time, under the banner of two hostile princes, waging a deadly war with each other. It is impossible to yield obedience to conflicting orders. No man can obey both God and Mammon. God says, "My son, give me thy heart." The prince of the power of the air, "shows us all the kingdoms of the world and the glory of them," and says to each one of us, "all these things will I give thee, if thou wilt fall down and worship me." God says, "the soul that sinneth, it shall die." Satan says, "take your fill of worldly pleasure, ye shall not surely die." God says, "all flesh is grass, and all the godliness thereof is as the flower of the field. The grass withereth, the flower fadeth; put not your trust in these vanishing things. Trust in the Lord for ever: for in the Lord Jehovah is everlasting strength." Mammon says, "Put your trust in this substantial world, 'for since the fathers fell asleep, all things continue as they were from the beginning of the creation.'" God says, "I dwell in the high and holy place, with him also that is of a contrite and humble spirit." Satan says, "Contrition is folly, humility is meanness. Fear not, 'thou dwellest in the clefts of the rocks, thou holdest the height of the hill, thou makest thy nest as high as the eagle; thou shalt never be brought down from thence.'" God says, "Ye are all as an unclean thing, and all your righteousnesses are as filthy rags. Do not place your hopes of salvation in your good deeds. Trust only in the name of the Lord Jesus. 'For there is none other name under heaven given among men, whereby ye must be saved.'" Satan reminds you of your fasting three times a week, of your giving tithes of all you possess, of your freedom from extortion, injustice, adultery, &c., and tells you "to look to the altars, the works of your hands, and have respect to that which your fingers have made." God calls "covetousness, idolatry," and pronounces "the love of money the root of all evil." Satan teaches that worldly wealth is the chief good—the noblest object of human desire. God says, "It is better to trust in the Lord than to put confidence in man." Satan teaches, "to love the praise of man more than the praise of God." God enjoins forgiveness of injuries—"Be ye kind to one another, tender-hearted, forgiving one another, even as God for Christ's sake has forgiven you." Satan prompts to "bitterness, and wrath, and anger, and clamour, and evil speaking with all malice."

It is impossible to obey such conflicting commands. Obedience must be rendered either to God or Mammon; but the same individual cannot obey both. Neither can he love both. Two masters, of like characters and of congenial dispositions, might be loved by the same servant. But the characters of God and Satan are as different as their respective abodes. "God is love." All his acts prove him to be long-suffering, merciful, and full of tender compassion. Satan is full of malice, hatred, cruelty, and murder. "He was a murderer from the beginning." God made man in his own image, pure, holy, and undefiled, and surrounded him with every object of delight. Satan defaced the image of God, banished him from Paradise, and sent him forth into a world of "thorns and thistles," cares and anxieties, sin and sorrow, disease and death. But notwithstanding the rebellion of man, "God" still "so loved the world that he gave his only begotten Son, that whosoever believeth in him should not perish, but have everlasting life." Satan visits the world too, but it is on no mission of mercy. He comes not as a Saviour, but a tempter.

> "Assaying by his devilish art to reach
> The organs of our fancy, and with them forge
> Illusions as he list, phantasms and dreams;
> At least distempered, discontented thoughts,
> Vain hopes, vain aims, inordinate desires,
> Blown up with high conceits, engendering pride."

God sends his "Spirit of truth, to guide into all truth." Satan sends his emissaries with "signs and lying wonders, and with all deceivableness of unrighteousness." Truth is an essential attribute of God. Titus i. 2. The throne of Satan is built on treachery and falsehood. "When he speaketh a lie, he speaketh of his own: for he is a liar, and the father of it." The tenderness of God for his people exceeds the love of the mother for her unweaned babe. "Can a woman forget her sucking child, that she should not have compassion on the son of her womb? Yea, they may forget, yet will I not forget thee." Isa. xlix. 15. Satan, too, forgets not, but he remembers only to destroy. "Your adversary, the devil, as a roaring lion, walketh about, seeking whom he may devour." 1 Pet. v. 8.

It is plain then, from this view of the opposite characters of God and Satan, that love for both cannot exist at the same time, in any human heart. If God be loved for his holiness, goodness, and truth, Satan must be hated for his wickedness, malevolence, and falsehood. If the service of the one be pleasant, the yoke of the other must be insufferable. The poor Pharisee, with his diseased eye, could not see this obvious truth. He sought to please God and win the world too. He sought to serve both God and Mammon. "How can ye believe," said our Saviour, "which receive honour one of another, and seek not the honour that cometh from God only"? The Pharisee coveted both, but he "loved the praise of men more than the praise of God." He gave to God the outer worship of tithes, mint, and cummin, and to Mammon the inner worship of the heart. But "God abhors the sacrifice, where not the heart is found." The mistake of the Pharisee of the time of our Saviour, is the mistake of the worldly Laodicean disciple of to-day. He strives to obey opposite and conflicting commands. He tries to love God, and yet not give up the love of the world. He wishes to save his soul and hoard his wealth too. He wants God to be his friend, and yet he withholds his substance from his service. He hopes that the great and dreadful Jehovah will accept the offering of his lips, while Mammon has the devotion of his soul. Let him listen to the truth from the lips of God's own Son—" Ye cannot serve God and Mammon."

NEEDLESS ANXIETY.

"Therefore I say unto you, Take no thought for your life, what ye shall eat, or what ye shall drink; nor yet for your body, what ye shall put on. Is not the life more than meat, and the body than raiment? Behold the fowls of the air: for they sow not, neither do they reap, nor gather into barns; yet your Heavenly Father feedeth them. Are ye not much better than they? Which of you by taking thought can add one cubit to his stature? And why take ye thought for raiment? Consider the lilies of the field, how they grow; they toil not, neither do they spin: and yet I say unto you, That even Solomon in all his glory was not arrayed like one of these. Wherefore, if God so clothe the grass of the field, which to-day is, and to-morrow is cast into the oven, shall he not much more clothe you, O ye of little faith? Therefore take no thought, saying, What shall we eat? or, what shall we drink? or, wherewithal shall we be clothed? (For after all these things do the Gentiles seek:) for your

Heavenly Father knoweth that ye have need of all these things." (Verses 25–32.)

We think that these verses do not contain additional reasons against the pursuit of worldly honour and worldly wealth—that which is called "treasure" in the 24th verse. The usually received opinion seems to us erroneous. It is not covetousness—greed for fame and riches—that our Saviour rebukes in the eight verses quoted above. It is needless anxiety about the necessaries of life, (food and raiment,) that he now condemns. He had shown, 1st. The folly of setting the heart on worldly objects, because of the insecurity of their possession; 2d. The sin of it, because the conscience was thereby defiled; and 3d. The danger of it, because the devotee of the world would cease to be a servant of God, and become the slave of Satan. He now passes to the consideration of what seems to be a lawful concern for those things which support existence. We are prone to think that it cannot be wrong to be concerned about providing the necessaries of life for ourselves and our families. Many, who are indifferent about the acquisition of wealth, are intensely solicitous about what they call a good support for their households. This solicitude our Saviour condemns, but not in the strong language of reprobation which is bestowed on the service of Mammon. Concern about food and raiment must be sinful, when it assumes the character "of a disquieting, tormenting care, which hurries the mind hither and thither, and hangs it in suspense; which disturbs our joy in God, and is a damp upon our hope in him, which breaks the sleep, and hinders our enjoyment of ourselves, of our friends, and of what God has given us." Again, this concern will be sinful when it assumes the character of "a distrustful, unbelieving thought. God has promised to provide for those that are his, all things needful for life as well as godliness, the life that now is, food, and a covering; not dainties, but necessaries. He never said they shall be feasted, but 'verily, they shall be fed.' Now, an inordinate care for time to come, and fear of wanting those supplies, spring from a disbelief of these promises, and of the wisdom and goodness of Divine Providence; and that is the evil of it. As to present sustenance, we may and must use lawful means to get it, else we tempt God; we must be diligent in our callings, and prudent in proportioning our expenses to what we have, and we must pray for 'daily bread;' and if all other means fail, we may and must ask relief of those that are able to give it. He was none of the best of men, who said, 'To beg, I am ashamed,' (Luke xvi. 3,) as he was, who (verse 21) 'desired to be fed with the crumbs which fell from the rich man's table.' But in regard to the future, we must 'cast our care upon God,' and 'take no thought,' for it looks like a distrust of God, who knows how to give what we want, when we know not how to get it." (*Matthew Henry.*)

This extract shows clearly that men may sin, even in their care for the necessaries of life. Distracting anxiety about anything, must interfere, not only with religious comfort, but also with religious duty. It dishonours God, too, by the distrust of his goodness and providence. Those, who are conscious that they are unconcerned about riches and honour, are not apt to think that they may offend God by over-anxiousness about the maintenance of their families. On the contrary, they rather think that they are to be commended for their solicitude, and their diligence in their business. They remember that the virtuous woman commended by Solomon, was distinguished for her industry, her thriftful management, and her wise forethought. They remember that diligence is always spoken of in the Scriptures with approbation, and that it is even enjoined as a duty. "He that gathereth in summer is a wise son." "The hand of the diligent maketh rich." "The hand of the diligent shall bear rule." "The thoughts of the diligent tend only to plenteousness." "Seest thou a man diligent in business, he shall stand before kings, he shall not stand before mean men." "Be thou diligent to know the state of thy flocks, and look well to thy herds." "Not slothful in business; fervent in spirit; serving the Lord." They remember, too, that idleness and slothfulness are spoken of in the severest terms of censure. And from all this, they infer that no tax upon the bodily and mental powers can be too great to provide a comfortable subsistence for themselves and their families. This opinion is confirmed in many, by the view generally taken of the eight preceding verses. They are commonly regarded as but the continuation of our Saviour's rebuke of an inordinate thirst for wealth and distinction. That this view is wrong, seems plain from the fact that distracting care about food and raiment, and not about wealth and fame, is that which is reproved. It is obvious, moreover, that bodily labour, even for the necessaries of life, may be carried to such an extreme, as to interfere with the offices of religion; such as family and secret prayer, visiting the sick, warning the impenitent, strengthening the weak, &c., &c. So, too, mental care, about food and raiment, may estrange the thoughts from God. We understand, then, our Saviour to pass, in the verses above, from a severe rebuke of covetousness, to a mild reproof of needless anxiety about a livelihood. He gives three reasons (verses 25, 26, 27,) against undue concern about food; three more (verses 28, 29, 30,) against undue concern about raiment; and then three more (verses 31, 32,) why we should not be troubled about either food or raiment.

We will notice these in their order. Food is mentioned first, because first in point of importance. Life may be, and has been maintained without clothing, but it cannot exist without food. This is implied in the very language employed in the 25th verse. "Take no thought for your *life*, what ye shall eat, or what ye shall drink; nor yet for your *body*, what ye shall put on." Here the contrast between the life and the body shows that food is essential, while raiment is but an ornament and a comfort.

The first argument against needless perplexity about food, is drawn from the superior dignity of life itself to the food that supports it. "Is not the life more than meat?" God has given the greater blessing, can you not trust him for the smaller? The greater boon was granted without your knowledge, without your care; why then bestow so much thought upon the smaller? The argument is of the same kind with that of St. Paul, where he expresses entire confidence in the love and goodness of God in *all* the affairs of life, because of the inestimable gift of his own Son, "He that spared not his own Son, but delivered him up for us all, how shall he not with him also freely give us all things?" Rom. viii. 32. Life is the breath of God. "The Lord God breathed into his nostrils the breath of life; and man became a living soul." Food is of the earth. Shall God give us a part of his own existence, and refuse us the vile, perishing things of earth? Would a prince give a jewel of priceless value to a favourite, and refuse the poor casket to keep it in. God has given us the nobler gift, let us trust him for the meaner. When we have bestowed all proper labour on our business, let us leave the issue with God, and disturb ourselves with no carking cares about the results of our efforts.

The second argument, against needless anxiety about food and raiment, is derived from God's care of the fowls of the air. "They sow not, neither do they reap, nor gather into barns; yet your Heavenly Father feedeth them. Are ye not much better than they?" (Verse 26th.) God cares for all his creatures, and makes provision for them all. "I know all the fowls of the mountains." Ps. l. 11. Not a sparrow can fall to the ground without his knowledge. Matt. x. 29. He "provideth for the raven his food, when his young ones cry unto God." Job xxxviii. 41. "He giveth to the beast his food, and to the young ravens which cry." Ps. cxlvii. 9. When God had resolved to destroy the world because of its wickedness, he did not forget the fowls of the air, but directed Noah to take them in by sevens of every kind. God has "made us wiser than the fowls of heaven." Job xxxv. 11. He has given us authority and dominion over them. Ps. viii. 8. If we find then that ample provision is made for the inferior creature, may not the nobler and more highly favoured, trust implicitly in the providence of God? There is a peculiar beauty in the illustration of our Saviour. The birds of the air make no provision for the future. They literally "take no thought for the morrow." The ant and the bee and many of the beasts of the field have a wise forecast, and lay up stores for winter. The squirrel does not forget, in the midst of his frisking and chattering on a bright summer day, to hoard away nuts for winter use. But the fowls of heaven, when their present wants are supplied, "sing among the branches," without any care, without any concern, without any thought, as to where the next supply is to come from. God is their provider, they have no reason to trouble themselves. He scatters food for them everywhere. The most careful reaper will leave much in the field for these "gleaners of the Lord." The most thrifty husbandman cannot store away his harvest, without leaving a portion to them. They come to the churl, as well as to the liberal man, for a part of his produce, and *they get it.* If then the most careless and improvident of all God's creatures be thus well supplied, shall the disciple of Christ perplex himself, saying, "What shall I eat? or, what shall I drink?" Let him labour faithfully, do his duty fully, and then trust for his food to Him who has charge of his soul. He will then be able to say with Paul, "I know whom I have believed, and am persuaded that he is able to keep that which I have committed unto him against that day;" or, with David, "I have been young and now am old, yet I have never seen the righteous forsaken, or his seed begging bread."

The third argument against distressing concern about food is drawn from our impotence and helplessness. "Which of you by taking thought can add one cubit to his stature." (Verse 27.)

The word rendered "stature" might have been rendered "age." It is so translated in several places. The parents of the blind man, when questioned by the Jews as to how he received his sight, replied, "he is of age, (*èlikian,*) ask him; he shall speak for himself." John ix. 21. "Through faith also Sarah herself received strength to conceive seed, and was delivered of a child when she was past age, (*èlikian,*) because she judged him faithful who had promised." Heb. xi. 11. The meaning then in this place is, who, by his care and anxiety in providing food, can add one cubit to his age? That is, who can lengthen his days by all the precautions that he may take to supply himself with the necessaries of life? "Is there not an appointed time for man upon earth?"

It has not been uncommon for the sacred writers, and for poets in ancient and modern times, to apply linear measure to time. Thus David: "Lord, make me to know mine end, and the measure of my days, what it is; that I may know how frail I am. Behold, thou hast made my days as an handbreadth, and my age (*elikia* in the Septuagint) is as nothing before thee." Ps. xxxix. 4, 5. Watts has beautifully versified one of the preceding thoughts:

"A span is all that we can boast,
An inch or two of time.

We understand then the drift of our Saviour's argument to be this: "Your great anxiety about food is in order to prolong your life. But none of you can add a single moment to the length of his existence. 'If ye then be not able to do that which is least, why take ye thought for the rest?' Luke xii. 26. If ye be not able to control a single instant, why take thought for the whole of life?" Our inability to lengthen the measure of our days, by even one second, should teach us the folly of troubling ourselves about what we shall eat and what we shall drink.

The first argument against useless anxiety about

raiment, is derived from God's care of the lilies of the field. "Consider the lilies of the field, how they grow; they toil not, neither do they spin: and yet I say unto you, That even Solomon, in all his glory, was not arrayed like one of these. Wherefore, if God so clothe the grass of the field, which to-day is, and to-morrow is cast into the oven, shall he not much more clothe you, O ye of little faith?" (Verses 28, 29, 30.) Our Saviour had shown the care bestowed by God upon his living, breathing, animate creatures; he now refers to his providence for the inanimate things that sprang into existence by the word of his power. There is thus a climax in his reasoning. The providence of God is more strikingly exhibited in his care for the senseless, unfeeling grass of the field, than in his providing for the singing, soaring birds of the air. His care for the latter might have been inferred from his care for the former. If he adorn and beautify the grass of the field, which is trodden down and eaten by the brute creation, shall he not much more care for the fowls of heaven, that warble hymns of praise to him all the day long? Then how much greater care will he give to man, who is nobler even than the blithesome caroling birds? We might have felt satisfied that God would not neglect us, inasmuch as he feeds the inferior living creatures; but all doubt must be banished, when we behold the attention bestowed on the soulless herbage at our feet. Mungo Park, the great African traveller, was once robbed and beaten, and left to perish in the wilderness. When he was just ready to resign himself to death, God suggested to him the very train of thought employed by our Saviour. He says: "At this moment, painful as my reflections were, the extraordinary beauty of a small moss caught my eye; and, though the whole plant was not larger than the top of my finger, I could not contemplate the delicate conformation of its roots, leaves, and fruit without admiration. 'Can that Being,' thought I, 'who planted, watered, and brought to perfection, in this obscure part of the world, a thing which appears of so small importance, look with unconcern on the sufferings of creatures formed after his own image? Surely not.' Reflections like these would not allow me to despair. I started up, and disregarding both hunger and fatigue, travelled forward, assured that relief was at hand, and I was not disappointed." We remember a similar exercise of faith (called forth in the same manner) by a traveller, lost on a prairie in Western Texas.

The reason of our Saviour's selection of this particular plant, the lily, for his illustration, was probably because it adorned the sides of the mountain on which he stood. All know that it was the common practice with our Saviour, to draw his illustrations from objects which presented themselves to the view of his hearers. Thus at Jacob's well, he talked to the woman of Samaria about the living water, which he who drank should thirst no more. And when he saw the multitudes from the city of Sychar coming to him across the fields, he said to his disciples: "Say not ye, there are yet four months and then cometh harvest? behold, I say unto you, Lift up your eyes, and look on the fields; for they are white already to harvest." And when he taught by the seaside, he said: "The kingdom of heaven is like unto a net, that was cast into the sea, and gathered of every kind. Which, when it was full, they drew to shore, and set down, and gathered the good into vessels, but cast the bad away." And in his last discourse, before his crucifixion, he said, as he passed among the clustering vines in the rich valley of the Cedron—"I am the true vine, and my Father is the husbandman. Every branch in me that beareth not fruit he taketh away; and every branch that beareth fruit, he purgeth it, that it may bring forth more fruit."

The beauty, simplicity, and power of our Saviour's teaching are due in great measure, to his constant practice of illustrating great moral truths by natural objects familiar to all. No religious teacher ever succeeded so well in divesting his instruction of a cold, dead, metaphysical abstraction, and in presenting it as a living, breathing reality, to the heart and the understanding. Ministers of the gospel would do well to imitate their Master in this, as well as in other respects. If they would study books less and nature more, they would not so often "speak in an unknown tongue" to the uneducated of their congregations. We think that it was Professor Wilson, of Edinburg, who said, that whenever he wished to make a great truth intelligible to the commonest comprehension, he endeavoured to recall the scenery around the country home of his childhood, so that he could employ a figure that would be felt and understood by all. Dead disquisitions on theology are too often substituted for the living, practical instruction, which our Saviour imparted. Our clergy are too much in their studies, and too little in the fields and in the forests. Nature is observed too little. "And if we do not observe nature, we incur disgrace as well as suffer loss—we are ungrateful to our Maker, and unworthy of ourselves. Wherefore were the organs and faculties of observation given us, if we do not use them. The senses (though, as we have them without cost, or study, or effort on our part, and so are apt to undervalue them,) are in reality choice gifts; and the productions of nature are so admirably fitted for the gratification of these senses, that it is altogether impossible for us not to perceive that the one must have been made for the other. Why does the rose give forth its odour, and the scent of the lavender and the mignonette steal viewless upon the still air around us, and the blooming bean, and the new mown hay, outscent all the preparations of the apothecary, if it be not to wile us to the garden and to the field, in order that we may breathe health, and at the same time cull pleasure and instruction there. Wherefore sings the breeze in the forest, why whispers the zephyr among the reeds, and how comes it that the caves and hollows of the barren mountains give out their tunes, as if the earth were a musical instrument of innumerable strings, if it be not to tempt us forth in order to learn how ever-fair, ever-new, and ever-informing, that great instructress is, who speaks to all the senses at one and the same instant." (*Mudie on Nature*, page 67.)

It is remarkable, that when God sought to recall Job from his murmuring and rebellion, it was done by pointing his attention to the wonders of creation. "Canst thou bind the unicorn with his band in the furrow? or will he harrow the valleys after thee? Gavest thou the goodly wings unto the peacocks? or wings and feathers unto the ostrich? Hast thou given the horse strength? hast thou clothed his neck with thunder? Doth the hawk fly by thy wisdom, and stretch her wings toward the south? Doth the eagle mount up at thy command, and make her nest on high? Canst thou draw out leviathan with a hook? or his tongue with a cord, which thou lettest down? He esteemeth iron as straw, and brass as rotten wood. The arrow cannot make him flee; sling-stones are turned with him into stubble. Upon earth there is not his like, who is made without fear."

And what was the effect upon Job of this contemplation of the handiwork of God? "Then Job answered the Lord and said, I know that thou canst do everything, and that no thought can be withholden from thee. . . . . Wherefore I abhor myself, and repent in dust and ashes."

We observe here, that it was the power, grandeur,

and majesty of God, as exhibited in his works, that convinced Job of his own folly and wickedness, in complaining of the dealings of so awful and glorious a Being. When, too, he reflected upon the wisdom, as well as power manifested in the structure of all of God's creatures, and contrasted that wisdom with his own ignorance, he felt that in complaining at God's providence he was but "darkening counsel by words without knowledge."

Religious teachers would do well to imitate the example of God the Father and God the Son, in illustrating moral truths by reference to the wonders of creation. It requires but little observation of nature

> "To find tongues in trees, books in the running brooks,
> Sermons in stones, and good in everything."

It may be well here, however, to notice the precise language employed by our Saviour. Why did he select the lily rather than any other flower of the field? Was it merely because it grew in beauty at his feet? This was doubtless the chief reason. Travellers tell us that the Eastern lily still abounds in Palestine. But there may have been an additional reason for the selection of this particular flower. The loveliness, fragrance, and lowliness of the Eastern lily made it a fit emblem of the Saviour himself. "I am," says he, "the rose of Sharon and the lily of the valleys." And he compares his Church to the lily among thorns. "As the lily among thorns, so is my love among the daughters." And God promises that his people shall grow as the lily in loveliness of character. "I will be as the dew unto Israel, he shall grow as the lily." Hosea xiv. 5. Now if we recollect that the Sermon on the Mount was addressed primarily to disciples, (Matt. v. 2,) we will have no difficulty in understanding why our Saviour made choice of the lily for his illustration of God's providence. He calls their attention to the care of their Heavenly Father for the lily, their emblem and representative. Will God care for the emblem and neglect the thing signified? Will he honour the type and disregard the antitype? Will he adorn and beautify the semblance and neglect the substance?

"Will God, think you, the just and great,
His meaner creatures bless,
And yet deny to man's estate
The boon of happiness?"

No, the loveliness of the symbol but prefigures the immortal bloom of the reality. If the lowly emblem be not forgotten, even when hidden among the thorns in the valley, but is arrayed in so gorgeous a drapery that Solomon's royal robes would be mean in the comparison, surely the child of God may trust him for suitable raiment in this world, and for glorious adornment in the life beyond the grave.

There is a peculiar significance in the fact that Christ likens himself to the rose and the lily, but compares his disciples to the lily alone. Song of Solomon ii. 1, 2. The lily is a bulbous plant. In the winter it does not lift its head above the ground, like the stately rose, but lies buried in the earth, and it may be, covered over with ice and snow. But when it feels the genial influence of the sun and the soft breath of spring, it bursts forth from its inglorious sepulture, and draws its rich colouring and variegated hues from the fountain of light and heat. And thus it is a fit emblem of one, whom the Father has given to the Son. He may be buried in worldly cares and worldly desires—he may be frozen under a cold, formal religion—but when the Sun of Righteousness has once shined into his soul, the cold and frost will disappear; and when the breath of God has blown upon the dry bones of his buried carcass, the man will start up in full, immortal vigour, and array himself in the glorious and refulgent robes of Immanuel's perfect righteousness.

The 32d verse contains three reasons against undue concern in regard to both food and raiment. 1st. Such concern is heathenish: "For after all these things do the Gentiles seek." 2d. We are not to trouble ourselves about these things, because we have God, and not Jupiter—not a heathenish deity, for our Father. "For *your* Heavenly Father." 3d. Because our situation and wants are perfectly known to this Father. "He knoweth that ye have need of all these things."

We propose to notice briefly these three reasons.

1st. Excessive concern about food and raiment is heathenish. The heathen had no correct ideas about the nature of God, and of course had none about his providential care over his creatures. The belief in a special providence was not entertained in any of their systems of philosophy. Two opinions prevailed with their sages. The first, that the gods were entirely indifferent to the affairs of men. The second, that the gods themselves were subordinate to the decrees of inexorable fate or fortune. The celebrated saying of Callisthenes is well known,

"Fortune, and not wisdom, rules the life of man."

Cicero taught that "fate or fortune governs everything." (See *Tusculan Disputations.*) The Roman empire was divided into two great schools—the Epicurean and Academic. The former taught that "if there were gods, they took no notice of human affairs;" the latter, that "it could not be ascertained whether there were gods or not; whether the soul was mortal or immortal; virtue preferable to vice," &c. (*McIlvaine's Evidences.*) The Greeks generally believed that the gods themselves were governed by fate. Of this belief Dr. Cudworth says, "There is another wild and extravagant conceit, which some of the Pagans had, who, though they verbally acknowledged a Deity, yet supposed Fate superior to it, and not only to all their petty gods, but also to Jupiter himself. To which purpose is the saying of the Greek poet, Latinized by Cicero, 'It is impossible for God himself to avoid the destined Fate. God himself is the servant of necessity.' According to which conceit, Jupiter, in Homer, laments his condition, in that the Fates have determined, that his beloved Sarpedon shall be slain by the son of Menetius, and that he is not able to withstand the decree. Though all these passages may not imply, perhaps much more than what the stoical hyothesis itself imported; for that did also, in some sense, make God himself the servant to the necessity of the matter, and to his own decrees, in that he could not have made the smallest thing in the world otherwise than it is now, much less was he able to alter it; according to that saying of Seneca, 'One and the same chain of necessity ties God and men. The same irrevocable and unalterable course carries on divine and human things. The very Maker and Governor of all things, that decreed the Fates, follows them. He did but *once* command, but he *always* obeys.'" (*Cudworth's Intellectual System of the Universe*, vol. i. page 54.)

It was of course impossible for the heathen, with their low views of the power of God, to trust him for their food and raiment. It was equally impossible for them, in their uncertainty about a future state, to be indifferent to the necessaries and comforts of the present life. The passing moment was everything to them. How could they be more concerned about their souls, whose very existence they doubted, than about their real, tangible, sensitive bodies? How could they commit the care of these bodies to deities whom they thought indifferent about them, or else bound like themselves in the chains of inflexible destiny? Anxiety about his bodily wants was natural to the heathen, but is sinful with the Christian, who has God for his Father and Provider.

The second argument, against undue concern about food and raiment—the necessaries of life, is drawn from this fact, of our having God for our Father. That child would be very foolish, who would perplex and distress himself about his food and clothing, although he knew that his kind father had abundant supplies at home, which he could get for the simple asking for them. The hungry prodigal turned his face homeward, when he remembered that in his father's house there was "bread enough and to spare." Luke xv. With how much more alacrity would he have hastened to the home of his childhood, had he known that his father was perfectly apprized of his hunger and suffering, and yearned to relieve his distress. And so we have the third argument as a climax to the whole. "Your Heavenly Father knoweth that ye have need of all these things." It would be enough to relieve the anxiety of any child, to know that he had a kind father near at hand, ready to supply everything asked for. But how much less anxiety ought that child to feel, if he knew that his tender parent never lost sight of him, and kept himself always acquainted with his wants, that he might anticipate them. Surely, it would be the height of folly, in such a child, to be troubled about his meat and his apparel. But the over-anxious Christian is just as foolish as the discontented child. "The Lord is good to all; and his tender mercies are over all his works." How much more shall they be over his chosen ones, washed and purified in the blood of his own Son. "He knoweth their down-sitting and their uprising; he understandeth their thoughts afar off. He compasseth their path, and their lying down, and is acquainted with all their ways." They have no wants which are not known to him. True, he may permit them to be naked and hungry, but it will never be from ignorance of their need; still less will it be from indifference to their suffering. He may have some wise purpose of discipline to accomplish thereby, or he may intend to exhibit them as models of patient endurance to a fretful and discontented world. Or, he may mean to make the more glorious their transition from a world of woe to a heaven of endless bliss. What a change for the poor beggar at the rich man's gate, from the company of dogs to Abraham's bosom; from squalid rags and a putrid carcass, to heavenly robes and a glorified body. Let the child of God then give himself no unnecessary concern, neither for wealth, nor for the necessaries of life. A kind and wise Father knows all his wants; and will supply or deny them, as seemeth to him best for the good of the child, and for the glory of his own great and holy name.

NEEDFUL ANXIETY.

"But seek ye first the kingdom of God and his righteousness; and all these things shall be added unto you." (Verse 33.)

This verse teaches us what we are to be anxious

for—what we may be lawfully concerned about. Two things may properly call forth and employ our thoughts and energies. We can never have too much solicitude about the kingdom of God and his righteousness—about the spread of the gospel of the Son of God, and our own personal holiness. We can never perplex ourselves too much to promote the glory of God, and to "work out our own salvation." Here is something worthy of our highest powers and most ardent zeal. Here is a work that, in its two-fold character, can engage man alone, of all the creatures in the great universe of God. Angels "faint not, neither are they weary" in their ceaseless efforts to glorify their blessed Creator. But angels are sinless beings—they have no heaven to win. They have not to seek the righteousness of a Surety and Substitute. God has made them perfectly holy and righteous in themselves, and they have not "left their first estate."

The transition from the eight preceding verses to the 33d verse, is quite natural. In the former, our Saviour teaches that there are two things, viz. food and raiment, not to be sought for with too much ardour. In the latter, he teaches that there are two things, viz. the glory of God, and personal holiness, which are to be striven for, with all eagerness and earnestness. And if we go still further back, these two lawful objects of the Christian's pursuit stand out in still broader contrast with the two things craved by the covetous, viz. wealth and fame. And all the arguments employed by our Saviour against covetousness, can be urged as reasons for concern about God's glory, and the soul's salvation. First, there can be no insecurity. No effort was ever lost, which was made in accordance with the teaching of God's word, to advance the Redeemer's kingdom, and to promote the sanctification of the man's own character. Whatever else may be uncertain, there is security here. However useless other exertions may be, these rest for their success upon the promise of a faithful and unchanging God. Second, there can be no perversion of conscience in the pursuit of these two grand objects. On the contrary, just in proportion as God is honoured and salvation sought for, will the understanding become enlightened, and the voice of conscience give true and faithful warning. Third, the man engaged in seeking first the kingdom of God and his righteousness, cannot enter into the service of Mammon. His noble employment will give him a distaste for the low, sordid desires and pursuits of the worldly. Moses, with his face all shining from his interview with Jehovah, could not fall down with his idolatrous brethren, before the image of the golden calf. Daniel but lightly esteemed the proffered chain of gold from the king of Babylon, because he looked forward to a crown of righteousness from the King of kings and Lord of lords.

Matthew Henry has shown that there are two reasons given for making the glory of God and our own personal salvation the chief objects of desire.

1st. These things are more worthy the attention of rational, immortal creatures, than provision for the wants of our poor perishing bodies. It will make but little difference, a little while hence, whether we were ill-fed in this life, and were clothed in rags, or were "clothed in fine linen and fared sumptuously every day;" whether we had hosts of friends, and were highly esteemed, or were deserted by all and left "alone like a sparrow upon the house-top." Elijah was probably never so happy as when he had but the company of the ravens by the brook Cherith. But it matters but little whether "the few and evil days of the years of our pilgrimage" be happy or miserable. This is but of small moment in comparison with the condition of the soul, which must "dwell in everlasting burnings," or enjoy full, supreme delight for ever and for ever. Of still less moment is it, in comparison with the glory of the eternal, self-existent God. 2d. "We have a surer and easier, a better and more compendious way to obtain the necessaries of this life, than by caring and fretting for them; and that is by seeking first the kingdom of God, and making religion our chief business." (*Matthew Henry.*) He has promised that all needed blessings shall be added to those who concern themselves more for his glory than for their own bodily wants. "And God said to Solomon, Because this was in thy heart, and thou hast not asked riches, wealth, or honour, nor the life of thine enemies, neither yet hast asked long life; but hast asked wisdom and knowledge for thyself, that thou mayest judge my people, over whom I have made thee king; wisdom and knowledge is granted unto thee; and I will give thee riches, and wealth, and honour, such as none of the kings have had that have been before thee, neither shall there any after thee have the like." 2 Chron. i. 11, 12. Solomon sought to honour God, first of all, because he desired to rule aright God's people; and personal blessings were therefore superadded. "Honour the Lord with thy substance, and with the *first-fruits* of all thine increase: so shall thy barns be filled with plenty, and thy presses shall burst out with new wine." "Trust in the Lord, and do good: so shalt thou dwell in the land, and *verily thou shalt be fed.*" "The Lord will give grace and glory: *no good thing will he withhold* from them that walk uprightly." "As the mountains are round about Jerusalem, so the Lord is round about his people from henceforth even for ever." "Blessed is every one that feareth the Lord; that walketh in his ways." "*For thou shalt eat the labour of thine hands:* happy shalt thou be, and it shall be well with thee." "The young lions do lack and suffer hunger: *but they that seek the Lord shall not want any good thing.*" "Godliness is profitable unto all things, *having promise of the life that now is*, and of that which is to come." The richness and fulness of these promises leave no room to doubt that God will attend to the temporal wants of those who are more concerned for his kingdom than for their own comforts and conveniences. The experience of every one must confirm the truth of these precious promises. It may be, indeed, that the child of God does occasionally perish from want. But doubtless his eternal happiness will be promoted by this light affliction, which is but for a moment. Has not a God of truth said, "all things work together for good to them that love God"?

GENERAL DIRECTION.

Having taught his disciples what two things they were to be concerned about, viz. God's glory and personal holiness, in opposition to the two things sought for by the covetous, viz. wealth and fame, and to the two things which troubled the Christian of "little faith," viz. food and raiment; our Saviour concludes with this general direction. "Take therefore no thought for the morrow; for the morrow shall take thought for the things of itself. Sufficient unto the day is the evil thereof." (Verse 34.)

This verse contains a command, and a twofold reason for compliance with it. The command is absolute. "Take no thought for the morrow;" more literally, do not *distract your mind* about the morrow. And the double reason is; 1st. To-morrow will have trouble enough of its own. Do not anticipate it. Do not neglect present duty by antedating future and inevitable calamity. 2d. To-day has evil enough of its own—sufficient to perplex us, to try our faith, and withdraw our thoughts from God. Let us not burden ourselves in addition, with the trials and difficulties that await us in the future. "Let us not pull that upon ourselves all at once, which providence has wisely ordered to be borne in parcels." (*Matthew Henry.*)

We will make a few comments upon the command, and the twofold reason annexed to it. We have seen throughout the whole discourse, that our Saviour never condemns a wrong without suggesting a remedy for it. The most effectual remedy against covetousness and needless anxiety about food and raiment, is entire unconcern about to-morrow. No man could possibly covet wealth and fame, no man could be greatly perplexed about the necessaries of life, who was regardless of the future. It is the thought of to-morrow that binds the servant of Mammon in strong and inflexible fetters. It is the thought of to-morrow that distresses the disciple of "little faith," when he reflects upon his slender means and inadequate resources. Our Saviour strikes at the root of the difficulty, when he positively forbids the distracting of our minds by thinking on the future; *not the future of weeks, and months, and years, but the future of to-morrow.* If harassing anxiety about even one day in advance, be peremptorily prohibited, how sinful must they be who neglect present service to God, while projecting into distant years their plans of ease, of wealth, and of honour. The whole scope of the Scriptures is opposed to man's prying into the future, and perplexing himself about his wants, either bodily or spiritual, beyond the mere supply of to-day.

"The secret things belong unto the Lord our God; but those which are revealed belong unto us and to our children." Deut xxix. 29. Does not he, who harasses himself about the future, trench upon the province of the God of heaven?

"To-morrow, Lord, is thine,
Lodged in thy sovereign hand,
And if its sun arise and shine,
It shines by thy command."

Under the Mosaic economy, the daily sacrifice taught daily dependence upon God. And so our Saviour directs us to say, "give us *this* day our daily bread." No supply is to be asked for beyond our immediate, pressing necessities. We must trust beyond the present moment to the Lord: "his compassions fail not. *They are new every morning.*" Lam. iii. 22, 23. Isaiah prayed that the Lord might be "their arm *every morning.*" Isa. xxxiii. 2. And God *will* give daily the support of his almighty arm to him who is willing to lean upon it. The Israelites were left without a guide in the pathless wilderness. But the pillar of cloud appeared every morning to conduct them on their journey. Night now shrouds the world in gloom and darkness, but we believe that to-morrow's sun will bring light and gladness. And thus the pillar of cloud and the mighty sun in the heavens are types of that goodness and mercy which are renewed every day. We trust God for light and guidance to-morrow, may we not also trust his guardian care in all the affairs of life? Undue solicitude about the future is foolish as well as sinful. Some, "through fear of death are all their lifetime subject to bondage." But why this fear? How do they know that they may not be cut down in a moment, or be insensible when the dread visitor shall make his approach? Thus it was in two instances in our own knowledge, of those who greatly feared death. How does the fearful know that when the dying hour shall come, dying grace will not be given? There are thousands of well-authenticated cases to prove that God will not desert his chosen ones, when "heart and flesh do fail them." Jesus, with the sins of the world upon him, felt, for a time, the hidings of his Father's face; but before he expired, he could utter the triumphant cry, "It is finished,"—"my great and glorious work is done." Poor, timid Cranmer, was all his lifetime subject to bondage from fear of death; but he was more than conqueror in the last trying moment.

"Jesus can make a dying bed,
Feel soft as downy pillows are."

Let us serve him when in health and strength; we need not fear that he will desert us in the hour of greatest need. We will then have something better to sustain us than the cold philosophy of the heathen warrior, who argued against the fear of death, that

"Cowards die many times before their deaths,
The valiant never taste of death but once."

Again, another looks with dread and horror upon the morrow, because of the dreariness and desolation that it will bring with it. The child of his bosom has been removed, the light of his house has been put out. Shall not to-morrow be as to-day, full of anguish and bitterness? Will it not come with its painful memories, its crushing heart-weight, its ever-abiding consciousness of the empty chair by the fire-side? Ah, to-morrow may well be dreaded! the stone of Sisyphus, that has been rolled up so wearily to-day, will be to roll up again to-morrow. But how do you know, bereaved parent, that your tenure of life is perpetual? How do you know that you may not be called in an instant to join your lost one? Why look forward gloomily to the morrow with its mourning and sorrow, when even now, the beloved arms may be stretched out to embrace you?

The conclusion then of the whole matter is, to do present duty well and faithfully, and leave the future to our wise and merciful Father. It will be in safe hands; we need not trouble ourselves about it.

Critical Exegesis. A more minute examination of a few words, in the last ten verses of the sixth chapter, deserves our attention. The word rendered "life," in the 25th verse, means also *soul*. Olshausen remarks, that this part of the discourse originates in a play upon this double meaning. The sensual man places the life-principle in sensual indulgence. But with the believer, the life is in the soul, and he "seeks first" its spiritual nourishment and support. In employing then this word, our Saviour tacitly rebukes the great concern for the perishing part, while indifferent to the immortal, undying part.

The word rendered, "take no thought" in this verse and also in the 31st and 34th verses, is a compound of three words; *not*, *split* or *divide*, and the *mind*. It then literally means do not split, divide, or distract the mind. The translation, "take no thought," is too strong, and does not convey the right idea. The same word is employed, in its participle form without the negation, in the 27th verse. And again as a verb, but without the negation, in the 28th verse. Many have taken the impression that our Saviour forbids all thought about worldly matters. He simply forbids that distracting care, which interferes with the right performance of religious duty, and amounts to a distrust of the providence of God. "Fowls of the *air*" might be rendered fowls of the *heaven*, and the immediate employment of the words, "your Heavenly Father," hints at the relationship of God to all his creatures. He is your Father, and also their Father; the locality assigned to him being the same as that assigned to them. The word, rendered "seek" in the 32d verse, (for after all these things do the Gentiles seek,) is a different one from that in the 33d verse, "seek ye first," &c. It is stronger in the 32d, and signifies seeking anxiously, intensely, with ardour. Doubtless, we are taught thereby how much more eagerly the carnal-minded seek the world than do the righteous the kingdom of heaven. "The children of this world are in their generation wiser than the children of light." Luke xvi. 8.

QUALIFICATION FOR REPROVING.

To understand the connection between the 7th chapter and the preceding, it is necessary to remember that our Saviour is now in that division of his discourse which treats of "what the disciples are not to be." They are here required not to be formalists like the Scribes and Pharisees; "for I say unto you, that except your righteousness shall exceed the righteousness of the Scribes and Pharisees, ye shall in no case enter into the kingdom of heaven." In this section of his sermon, our Saviour first shows the doctrinal errors of these religious sects, and then their errors of practice. The exposure of their doctrinal errors closes with the 5th chapter, and then with the 1st verse of the 6th chapter, begins the exhibition of their sins of practice. These are shown to be three-fold. They did not perform the duty they owed to God, nor to themselves, nor to society. 1st. They failed in their duty to God; (shown from 1st verse to 19th.) They sought to promote their own fame, and not the glory of God, by their almsgiving, fasting, and prayer. 2d. They were false to their duty to themselves; (shown from 19th verse to the close of chapter vi.) Instead of attending to their highest interests, those which pertained to their undying souls, they were concerned only about their perishing bodies. They were devoted to the service of Mammon, and were constantly inquiring, "What shall we eat? and wherewithal shall we be clothed?"

And now, in the 7th chapter, we have exhibited their dereliction of duty towards their fellow-creatures. Instead of exercising towards them that "charity, which suffereth long and is kind," they were bitter, harsh, and censorious in their judgments and opinions. In a word, "they trusted in themselves that they were righteous, and despised others." Luke xviii. 9. And thus our Saviour gives a faithful picture of Pharisaism; shows it to be wrong in doctrine, and wrong in practice; wrong in its instruction of others, wrong in its own performance.

With these preliminary observations to establish the connection between the 7th chapter and the two chapters which precede it, we will proceed to examine the following verses.

"Judge not, that ye be not judged. For with what judgment ye judge, ye shall be judged; and with what measure ye mete, it shall be measured to you again. And why beholdest thou the mote that is in thy brother's eye, but considerest not the beam that is in thine own eye? or how wilt thou say to thy brother, Let me pull the mote out of thine eye; and, behold, a beam is in thine own eye? Thou hypocrite, first cast out the beam out of thine own eye; and then shalt thou see clearly to cast out the mote out of thy brother's eye." (Verses 1—5.)

Our Saviour gives us here a rule, and the penalty for its non-observance. The rule is "judge not," and the penalty for not observing it, is incurring a like judgment to that we exercise. We will refer to a separate section the consideration of the rule, and the punishment for neglecting it; and notice first the qualification required in reprovers. Two species of judging are contemplated. The first (treated of in the 3d verse) contents itself with being sharp-sighted enough to see the mote in a brother's eye, while blind to the beam in its own. The second (treated of in 4th verse) may not be more malignant than the first, but it is more presumptuous, more officious, more intermeddling. It is not satisfied with finding the mote, it is keen to pull it out. It is a fanatical reformer. It wishes to set the world to rights. The beam in its eye has made it far-sighted. It sees hideous sins a great way off, but it cannot perceive the corruption at home. The silent phase of judging of the 3d verse, is ever first in order of time. It is the gathering of the thunder clouds before the ravage and desolation of the storm. It is the marshalling the hosts and planting the artillery, before the shock and carnage of the battle. The meddling phase prompts to intolerance, persecution and murder. It established the Inquisition. It covered "the Alpine mountains cold" with the bones of the saints of God. It drenched the valleys of Piedmont with their heart's blood. It butchered ninety thousand Huguenots in a single night. It kindled the fires of Smithfield. It drove to the wilds of America the chosen ones of the Most High. It invented thumb-screws, iron boots, and ten thousand instruments of torture, to maim, and mangle, and murder the heirs of God and joint-heirs of Jesus Christ, "of whom the world was not worthy." It is still active, rampant, ruthless, remorseless, ravening for blood. It is found wherever fanatics do congregate, prompting them to say to their friends and neighbours, "stand aside, we are holier than you." It is now putting forth all its hellish powers to array one section of our glorious union against another; to fill the hearts of the common inheritors of the freedom won by common ancestors, with hatred, malice, and wrath towards each other.

Such are the two forms of judging mentioned in the 3d and 4th verses. We may designate them as the silent-malignant, and the meddling-malignant. They stand to each other in the relation of parent and child, fountain and stream, cause and effect. The silent-malignant fills the heart of the censorious with ill-will and enmity towards his neighbour, and naturally ends in the meddling-malignant, which seeks to reform him. But if the man be unwilling to be reformed, if he refuse to have the mote pulled out of his eye, if he deny that there is any mote there, then the meddling-malignant is ready with dungeons and cells, racks and stocks, gibbets and stakes, either to bring the refractory to terms, or to punish him for his contumacy. And thus has arisen every species of persecution that has filled our world with lamentation and woe, misery and bloodshed. All have had their root in a fault-finding, censorious spirit, which judged rashly and harshly the religious sentiments and characters of others. All private feuds, quarrels and frays, which have destroyed the happiness of individuals, and the peace of society, have originated, with scarcely an exception, in precisely the same way.

Our Saviour most emphatically condemns both forms of harsh judging; the silent-malignant and the meddling-malignant. But he bestows an epithet of contempt, "thou hypocrite," (verse 5,) upon the officious fault-finder, which he does not inflict upon the man of silent malevolence. He, who was most free to rebuke others, most deserved rebuke himself. In administering this rebuke, Christ gives us a rule by which we may judge of our qualifications to turn censors upon the conduct of others. The rule is thus expressed by himself; "first cast out the beam out of thine own eye, and then shalt thou see clearly to cast out the mote out of thy brother's eye." Nothing can be plainer than this direction. *The man who sets up to reprove others must himself be sinless.* And the figure employed by our Saviour contains the strongest possible reason why the rule should be just as it is. The man who has a beam, or a mote even, in his own eye, cannot see clear enough to pull out the mote from his brother's eye. So the man who has any sin in his heart, will have his judgment so warped, and his opinions so biassed, that he is incapable of forming a just estimate of his neighbour's character. What is most lovely in that character may seem to him most odious and censurable. The Jews could see "no form nor comeliness" in the Son of God. Sinners can see none now. Sin darkens the understanding and perverts the judgment. It utterly disqualifies us from measuring aright the motives and principles of others.

The saints of the Most High have of all men been the most hated and persecuted. They have "had trial of cruel mockings and scourgings, yea, moreover of bonds and imprisonments: they were stoned, they were sawn asunder, were tempted, were slain with the sword: they wandered about in sheep-skins and goat-skins; being destitute, afflicted, tormented." Heb. xi. 36, 37. The worst of men have been the most caressed and flattered by the world. "Woe unto you," said the Son of God, "when all men speak well of you." All this proves, that man in his sin-darkened condition, is unfit to pass judgment upon his neighbour's conduct; and he is therefore wisely forbidden to exercise reproof. The smallest degree of personal guilt impairs the faculty of judging aright, so that only a perfectly holy being is qualified to perceive and rebuke the faults of others. "Let him that is *without sin* among you first cast a stone at her," was the reply of our blessed Redeemer to a crowd of meddling-malignants, thirsting for the blood of a woman, no more guilty than themselves. In exact accordance with this rule of our Saviour, does St. Paul define the qualifications of the censor: "Thou therefore which teachest another, teachest thou not thyself? thou that preachest, a man should not steal, dost thou steal? thou that sayest a man should not commit adultery, dost thou commit adultery? thou that abhorrest idols, dost thou commit sacrilege? thou that makest thy boast of the law, through breaking the law dishonourest thou God?" Rom. ii. 21–23. Here we are plainly told that no one has a right to rebuke others for sins which he himself commits. But on another occasion, St. Paul goes still further, and not only excludes from the office of censor, all who are now indulging in sin, but all who have ever sinned. "Put them in mind to be subject to principalities and powers. . . . . To *speak evil of no man*, to be no brawlers, but gentle, showing all meekness to all men. *For we ourselves were also* sometimes foolish, disobedient, deceived, serving divers lusts and pleasures, living in malice and envy, hateful and hating one another." Titus iii. 1–3. Here we are absolutely forbidden to speak evil of any man, and the reason given for it is that we ourselves have been transgressors. The recollection of past offences should make us humble, should subdue that pride and self-complaisance which prompts to intolerance of the faults of others. If we were all more ready to search out the corruptions of our own hearts, than to pry into the failings of our acquaintances, the cry "God be merciful to me a sinner," would oftener be heard, than "see how wicked my neighbour is." The rule of our Saviour and that of St. Paul, taken in connection, grant the privilege of censuring others, to those alone who are sinless, and have ever been so. If it were exercised only by those, there would be no more gossiping, no more tattling, no more scandal-mongering, no more wrangling, no more quarreling, no more persecution. Fanaticism would lose its power to hurt and destroy. Feuds and frays, wars and rumours of wars would come to an end. Peace and good-will toward God and man would cover the whole earth, as the waters cover the sea. Arsenals would be turned into work-shops, and the implements of destruction into the tools of the artisan and husbandman.

The question then may be asked, have we no right to form opinions of others, so that we may be able to select our associates and friends? Surely we have; and we are directed how to form our opinion of them. "By their fruits shall ye know them." We have a right to form our estimate of men by the fruits of their lives—by their external conduct. We may judge of their actions, but we may not judge of the motives to those actions. "The secret things belong unto the Lord our God." It is presumptuous, then, to go beyond the outward manifestation, and seek to pry into the secret spring of action. The deeds of men give a fair test of their character, and we need no other. "Can a corrupt tree bring forth good fruit?" Hence, without going beyond the test given us, we may question a seemingly good deed from a man of known bad character. We judge of a tree by its yield during a succession of years, not by a single bearing. And here we would enter the caution, that though we are permitted, for our guidance in social intercourse, to judge men by their outward conduct, yet should that judgment be unfavourable, we have no right to blazon it abroad; only when called upon by the civil authorities, or when urged by a sense of duty to warn friends against a dangerous character, may we with propriety make our opinion known. Dr. Brown says, "I apprehend that the command, 'Speak evil of no man,' requires us steadily to avoid giving an opinion to a man's disadvantage to any one but to himself, except when duty demands it." (*Brown's Exposition, page* 251.) And though circumstances may warrant the divulging of an adverse opinion of our neighbour, they will not, of course, excuse us, should that opinion have been hastily and uncharitably formed.

Magistrates and rulers are allowed more latitude in regard to reproving. They are the vicegerents of God upon earth. "The powers that be, are ordained of God." "By me princes rule, and nobles, even all the judges of the earth." Those in authority, then, are not forbidden to judge and speak evil, simply because God has delegated this prerogative to them. They may lawfully censure and condemn, and their voice of admonition and rebuke should be as the voice of God. "Rulers" should be "a terror to evildoers." They are, of course, then, permitted to reprove and punish. "But woe unto them that decree unrighteous decrees, and that write grievousness, which they have prescribed." Isa. x. 1. "Cursed be he that perverteth the judgment of the stranger, fatherless and widow. And all the people shall say Amen." Deut. xxvii. 19. "Thou shalt not wrest judgment; thou shalt not respect persons, neither take a gift; for a gift doth blind the eyes of the wise, and pervert the words of the righteous." Deut. xvi. 19. The ruler who makes an unjust decree, and the magistrate who wrests judgment, not only wrong their fellow-creatures, but also tarnish the glory of God; just as unworthy ambassadors dishonour the governments which they represent. And just here lies the only true ground of rebellion against constituted authority. Wicked rulers have forfeited their character as the representatives of God. They are no longer his delegates; and the question of submission or resistance to their mandates, becomes simply a question of expediency, and not of conscience. And thus we justify the English rebellion of 1649 and that of 1688; the revolt of the Netherlands in 1572; our own Revolution in 1776; the unsuccessful insurrection in Mexico, under Hidalgo, in 1810; the overthrow of the Spaniards by Iturbide in 1821; the dethronement of Iturbide himself in 1824; the expulsion of the Spaniards from South America, 1821–6, &c., &c.

Ministers of the gospel, in their official character, are probably exempt altogether from the penalty annexed to judging others. Their vocation is of reproof, as well as of warning and exhortation. They are the mouth-pieces of the Most High, and their messages, delivered in his fear, should be as the oracles of the living God. But even this privileged class of men are directed to mingle charity and forbearance with their censure. "Reprove, rebuke, exhort *with all long-suffering and doctrine.*" "In *meekness* instructing those that oppose themselves." Even Moses was not allowed to use harsh language to the rebellious Israelites. Because "he spake unadvisedly with his lips," he was not permitted to enter into the promised rest.

Parents, masters, teachers, and all who are acting as delegates of God, may, in that capacity, judge and execute sentence, provided that they do so with all due deliberation, with all Christian charity and with all due consideration. But all who are hasty to form harsh opinions of others in their own hearts, and are rash to express their opinions when not called upon by the civil authorities or by a sense of duty, violate the precept of our Saviour, and are liable to the punishment annexed to that violation. There is no precept of our Master more frequently and more flagrantly violated than this in respect to judging. The chief cause of it is doubtless to be found in the depravity of human nature; but it may also proceed, in part, from a misinterpretation of the privilege granted to us, of judging men by the fruits of their lives. Some honestly believe that the privilege virtually abrogates the precept, and think that when forming the most uncharitable opinions of men's motives, they are only judging them by their fruits. This is plainly a perversion. The tree is to be judged by the fruit, not by the hidden juices and concealed processes of vegetation. So the man is to be judged by his outward conduct, and not by the secret workings of his heart. We understand the command, "judge not," to refer especially to judgment of motives—just the sort of judgment which the men of the world pass, when they pronounce all religion hypocrisy—just the sort of judgment bigots pass, when they regard all denominations corrupt except their own—just the sort of judgment proud Pharisees pass, when they look with scorn upon poor Publicans worshipping afar off. The visible conduct may be judged, and if we feel aggrieved by it, we have ample directions given us how to act. Matt. xviii. 15–17. These, it is needless to say, do not warrant us in publishing abroad our neighbour's transgressions.

RETRIBUTION.

"For with what judgment ye judge, ye shall be judged; and with what measure ye mete, it shall be measured to you again." (Ver. 2.) Our Saviour gave two reasons against harsh judgment of the principles and character of others. 1st. That we thereby incur the displeasure of God, and that he will deal with us as we have dealt with our neighbours. 2d. That we are incapable of judging aright with our sin-darkened understandings.

It suited our purpose better to consider the second reason first; we will now examine the first reason. The main idea here is, that the treatment we give, or *meditate* to give others, God will give to us. Our happiness for time and for eternity is in our own hands. Each of us holds a measuring rod, more powerful than the magic wand of Mercury, more wonderful than the staff of Moses, that confounded the wise men of Egypt. It is a rod with which we are meting out every moment our weal or our woe for all eternity. The wand of Mercury had no power over the superior gods; but this (with reverence be it spoken) seems to influence even the great God of heaven; for just as we treat him, will he treat us. He loves them that love him. Prov. viii. 17. With the merciful he will show himself merciful, and with the upright man he will show himself upright. With the pure he will show himself pure; and with the froward he will show himself unsavoury. 2 Chron. xxii. 25, 26. If in time of health and prosperity we set at naught his counsel and will have none of his reproof, he will also laugh at our calamity, and mock when our fear cometh. Prov. i. 25, 26. How strange it seems, that the great Author of an infinite system of worlds should measure his conduct by that of a poor creature, who is but a speck on the surface of one of these worlds. And yet such is the teaching of God's Holy Word. It is his law that men shall be the authors of their own happiness or their own misery, both in this life and that which is to come. Let the circumstances by which two men are surrounded be precisely the same, and yet the one will be happy and the other wretched. The poet has truly said,

. . . "From out the self-same fount
One nectar drank, another draughts of gall.
Hence, from the self-same quarter of the sky,
One saw ten thousand angels look and smile;
Another saw as many demons frown;
One discord heard, where harmony inclined
Another's ear. The sweet was in the taste,
The beauty in the eye, and in the ear
The melody; and in the man—(for God
Necessity of sinning laid on none)—
To form the taste, to purify the eye
And tune the ear, that all he tasted, saw
Or heard, might be harmonious, sweet and fair."

The experience of every man must confirm the truth of the above statement. And the philosophy of it is to be found in this, that men get the very measure which they give or meditate to give to others. Thus, the kind and gentle are generally treated with great kindness and gentleness. Even the contentious are constrained to be courteous to them. "For a soft answer turneth away wrath." The irascible and irritable, on the contrary, excite the anger and indignation of their associates. Thus, too, the haughty and supercilious, who lightly esteem others, are but lightly esteemed themselves. But the meek and lowly are held in high repute. Thus, too, the liberal man meets with unbounded generosity, while the churlish miser is reckoned with to the last farthing. Thus, too, the vainglorious babbler who chatters away to show his superiority to others, is esteemed a fool. But "even a fool, when he holdeth his peace, is counted wise; and he that shutteth his lips is esteemed a man of understanding." Thus, too, the mischief-maker, who is constantly devising evil for others, is ever in trouble himself. "Whoso diggeth a pit shall fall therein; and he that rolleth a stone, it will return upon him." Prov. xxvi. 27. "The heathen are sunk down into the pit that they made; in the net which they hid is their own foot taken." Ps. ix. 15. Who is so frequently maligned and misrepresented as the slanderer? "A false witness shall not go unpunished, and he that speaketh lies shall not escape." Prov. xix. 5. "They whet their tongue like a sword, and bend their bows to shoot their arrows, even bitter words; that they may shoot in secret at the perfect; suddenly do they shoot at him, and fear not. But God shall shoot at them with an arrow; suddenly shall they be wounded. *So shall they make their own tongue to fall upon themselves.*" Ps. lxiv. Here we are taught that the slanderer is punished in the same manner and with the same weapons that he punished others with. Thus, too, with men of blood—they are almost invariably made to fill bloody graves. How true it is, that "bloody and deceitful men shall not live out half their days." Ps. lv. 23. Though they may escape the penalty of the law, they cannot fly from the vengeance of God. So common a thing has been the untimely death of the murderer, that it has not failed to attract the notice even of the heathen. When Paul, after his shipwreck, stood warming himself by the fire on the island of Melita, a "viper came out of the heat and fastened on his hand. And when the barbarians saw the venomous beast hang on his hand, they said among themselves, No doubt this man is a murderer, whom though he hath escaped the sea, yet vengeance suffereth not to live." Acts xxviii. 3, 4. This was, doubtless, not a mere superstition with the barbarians, but the result of experience. They had, no doubt, observed the frequency with which men of blood have been suddenly cut off in their wickedness. The observation of the whole world confirms the same thing. In fact it has passed into a proverb that "murder will out." Since the day that Abel fell by the hand of his brother, blood, by whomsoever shed, crieth unto the Lord from the ground. And the wretched homicide is cursed from the earth, that has opened her mouth to receive the victim's blood. Gen. iv. 10, 11.

We have many instances both in sacred and profane history of retributive justice. We only notice a few of them.

The Israelites after the death of Joshua, fought against, conquered and captured Adoni-Bezek, the lord of Bezek. They cut off his thumbs and great toes. This was not an uncommon punishment in those days, nor in fact for many ages after. It was done to incapacitate the captive for the use of the javelin and the sword, and to unfit him for marches and campaigns. This, however, is the only instance in the sacred record, of so barbarous a punishment; and mark the reason: "And Adoni-Bezek said, Threescore and ten kings, having their thumbs and great toes cut off, gathered their meat under my table; *as I have done, so God hath requited me.*" Jacob lied to his father and defrauded his brother of his heritage. Laban defrauded him of the wife for whom he had laboured seven years. His own sons lied to him, as he had lied to his father. And as it was the partiality of his mother for him that led him to deceive Isaac, and wrong Isaac's favourite; so it was his own partiality for Joseph that induced his sons to wrong their father's favourite and deceive himself. Saul fell by his own hand, the hand that so often sought to slay David. Ahab, at the instigation of his wicked wife, Jezebel, caused Naboth to be put to death, so that he might get his vineyard. But Elijah met him, as he was going down to take possession of his blood-bought treasure. "Hast thou killed and also taken possession. Thus saith the Lord, 'In the place where dogs licked the blood of Naboth shall dogs lick thy blood, even thine.' And of Jezebel also spake the Lord, saying, The dogs shall eat Jezebel by the wall of Jezreel." These predictions were fulfilled to the very letter. Daniel was thrown into a den of lions through the malice of his enemies. But God "sent his angel and shut the lions' mouths." And the king, Darius, commanded that the accusers of Daniel should be thrown into the same den. "And the lions had the mastery of them and brake all their bones in pieces or ever they had touched the bottom of the den." The Hebrew youths, Shadrach, Meshach and Abed-nego, escaped the heat of the fiery furnace unscathed, but those that threw them in perished by the flame. Haman, to signalize his vengeance against Mordecai, prepared for him a gallows fifty cubits high. He was himself suspended from that lofty height, a monument to the whole city of Shusan of the retributive justice of God. The Jews sold our Saviour for thirty pieces of silver, the price of a slave, and then crucified the Lord of glory. We are told that they themselves were sold into slavery until no purchasers could be found, and were crucified until "wood was wanting with which to make crosses."

Profane as well as sacred history is full of instances of fearful retribution, attending actual or contemplated crimes. Thus we read that Pope Alexander VI. prepared a jar of poisoned sweet-meats, with which to destroy the wealthy Cardinal Corneto. He ate of them himself and died in agony. Louis, the Debonnaire, son and successor of Charlemagne, put his nephew Bernard to death, and forced his *three* natural brothers to assume the clerical tonsure. This was done at the instigation of his queen. She died, and he married again. His second wife was unfaithful and gave birth to a spurious son. His own *three* sons treated him as unnaturally as he had treated his *three* brothers, and finally the spurious child succeeded to the empire of France. So that all of Louis's crimes to secure France to his descendants were completely frustrated, and he gained nothing but a similar unnatural treatment, to that which he had shown. Anne Boleyn, maid of honour to queen Catherine, encouraged the addresses of Henry VIII., and thereby stimulated him to divorce his lawful wife. When Catherine died of grief and mortification, Anne could not conceal her exultation, and said that she was then a queen indeed. But at that very moment, repayment in kind was awaiting the rejoicing queen. The lustful monarch had looked with unhallowed love upon Jane Seymour, one of *her own* maids of honour, and Anne was brought to the block to make way for *her* rival. But justice was not merely meted out to the wretched Anne. Cardinal Wolsey, who conspired against Catherine and encouraged Henry to divorce her, was himself soon after disgraced and divorced from all his wealth and dignity. Cranmer, who was active in the same wicked deed, but from different motives from Wolsey, was burned years after by the daughter of the disgraced queen. Mary thirsted for the blood of the man who had wronged her mother, and her hatred of Cranmer more than her love of Catholicism brought him to the stake. Napoleon divorced the noble Josephine, so that the crown of France might be transmitted to his own descendants. A grandson of the divorced queen is now on the throne, and the race of Napoleon Buonaparte is extinct. The imperious and vindictive Sarah cast out Hagar and Ishmael into the wilderness, saying "the son of this bond-woman shall not be heir with my son, even with Isaac." But all that country is now possessed by the descendants of the bond-woman, while the children of Isaac are scattered over the face of the whole earth.

And what is the history of the different dynasties that have tyrannized over mankind, but the record of murder and usurpation, and then in turn, dethronement and death? They sprung up in blood, and they went out in blood. What a black catalogue of crimes do the histories of the Assyrian and Persian empires present. Treason and assassination, and then fearful retribution by the dagger or poisoned bowl, upon the traitors themselves; these constitute almost one-half their annals. It is but little better in modern history. We have the same circle; beginning in conspiracy and murder, and coming back to the starting point of conspiracy and murder. We meet this bloody round of treachery and vengeance again and again in England, during the dark era of the "war of the roses." Edward IV. and his brutal brothers murdered Henry VI., the Prince of Wales, and thousands of the adherents of the house of Lancaster. And then the royal trio turned their fury against one another. Clarence was murdered by his brothers. Edward perished in the prime of his life; his death being hastened by the cares and anxieties attending the usurped crown, by remorse for his brother's death, and by his indulgence in those pleasures which his assumed rank gave him. His two sons were murdered by command of their uncle Richard, and Richard himself was slain in battle. And nearly all who aided the fierce brothers in their cruelties, came to untimely ends.

It is remarkable how few great conquerors have died natural deaths. Alexander the Great perished in his thirty-third year; it matters but little whether by *poison* (as some suppose) or by excess in drinking. In either case, his conquests led to his death; for his career of victory brought about him a crowd of sycophants, who paid him the most idolatrous homage and encouraged him in his excesses. Hannibal destroyed himself by poison, to escape from falling into the hands of his enemies. Cæsar fell beneath the daggers of his former friends, in the Senate house of Rome. Napoleon died in his fifty-second year; his death being hastened by his confinement, by mortification at the loss of his power, and by the vexatious treatment to which he was subjected. Charles XII. was killed by a cannon ball. Gustavus Adolphus fell in battle on the plains of Lutzen; even that virtuous monarch forming no exception to the law, "He that killeth with the sword must be killed by the sword." The greatest of warriors, Marshal Turenne, was killed by a cannon ball at Saltzbach. The brutal Suwarroff died of a broken heart because of the neglect of his royal master, Paul. A similar fate was that of Gonsalvo de Cordova, "the Great Captain," as the Spaniards still delight to call him. He died in retirement, an exile from court and under the displeasure of his sovereign. The declining years of Cortes were embittered by the malice and envy of his enemies. Alvarado, his lieutenant, who won such an enviable notoriety for his cruelty and rapacity, filled at length a bloody grave. The remorseless Francisco Pizarro fell by the hands of wretches as pitiless as himself. Diego Almagro, who had signalized himself by his cruelty to the Peruvian monarch, Atahualpa, was strangled to death whilst a prisoner. And so hundreds of other instances might be given, to show that God does avenge the shedding of the blood of those made in his own image.

Parallel to the fate of warriors and conquerors is that of tyrants and wicked rulers. How few of these have been permitted to live out half their days! The licentious monster, Domitian, fell by the hand of the assassin. The fiddling fool and bloody knave, Nero, poisoned himself. The ferocious Caligula was killed by conspirators, after a reign of four years. The brutal Commodus was first poisoned and then strangled. The savage fratricide, Caracalla, was stabbed with a dagger. The effeminate, superstitious, vindictive Elagabalus, was assassinated by the Pretorian guards. The remorseless giant, Maximin, was slain in his tent. The cruel debauchee, Gallienus, was killed by a dart from the hand of a conspirator. Carinus, who, Gibbon says, united the extravagances of Elagabalus with the cruelties of Domitian, fell by the hand of an injured husband. Gallus, distinguished for his treachery and blood-thirstiness, was betrayed and murdered, &c., &c. And if we come down to the darkest and most disgraceful of all the periods in history, the era of the French Revolution, what a commentary is afforded on the text, "As thou hast done, it shall be done to thee; thy reward shall return upon thine own head." Obadiah 15. How few of the traffickers in blood were permitted to close their lives in peace! How fearful was the retribution upon the ruthless triumvirate, Danton, Marat and Robespierre. Danton was sentenced to the guillotine by the *very revolutionary tribunal which he himself had established.* Marat was stabbed to the heart by Charlotte Corday. She pretended that she had important information respecting his intended victims in Caen, and thus got access to his person. "She found him in the bath, where he eagerly inquired after the proscribed deputies at Caen. Being told their names, 'they shall soon meet the punishment they deserve,' said Marat. 'Yours is at hand,' said she, and stabbed him to the heart." (*Alison.*) And thus he fell with murder in his heart, and the words of death on his lips. The vengeance of Heaven on Robespierre, the greatest monster of the three, was still more signal. His lower jaw was shattered by a pistol ball; he was then dragged by the heels over the pavements into his own quarters, and *laid on the very table on which he had signed so many death-warrants.* There he lay for nine hours, enduring agony unutterable from his wound, half frantic with terror of death, and cowering under the jeers and taunts of the mob. He was next taken to the *very cell* in which he had a few days before confined some of his victims. At 4 o'clock next morning he was taken to the scaffold, *erected on the very spot* where his royal victims, Louis XVI. and Maria Antoinette, had been executed. "The blood from his jaw burst through the bandage and overflowed his dress; his face was deadly pale. He shut his eyes, but could not close his ears against the imprecations of the multitude. A woman, breaking from the crowd, exclaimed, 'Murderer of all my kindred, your agony fills me with joy; descend to hell, covered with the curses of every mother in France.' Twenty of his comrades were executed before him; when he ascended the scaffold, the executioner tore the bandage from his face; the lower jaw fell upon his breast, and he uttered a yell which filled every heart with horror. For some minutes the frightful figure was held up to the view of the multitude; he was then placed under the axe, and the last sounds which reached his ears were their exulting shouts, which were prolonged for some minutes after his death. 'Yes, Robespierre, there is a God!' said a man, approaching the lifeless body of one so lately the object of dread. His fall was felt by all present as an immediate manifestation of the Divinity." (*Alison.*) The butcher, Couthon, was guillotined. So was his colleague, the sanguinary atheist, St. Just.

After the deaths of Marat and Danton, Couthon and St. Just with Robespierre constituted the second revolutionary triumvirate. They suffered with him on the *same* spot where the royal family had suffered, and where the allied sovereigns, on their mission of vengeance and retribution, "took their station, when their victorious armies entered Paris, on the 31st of March, 1814." Farquier-Tinville, the public accuser, probably the blackest hearted villain of them all, was brought to the block (soon after the fall of Robespierre,) amid the execrations of an immense multitude. Hebert, one of the most pitiless of all "the terrorists," the projector of the "feasts of reason," in contempt of religion and a future state, manifested the utmost terror, when his own head was brought under the revolving axe. Some of the terrors of that after life, which he had affected to disbelieve, were made by retributive justice to be his portion even in this. The "first apostle of liberty," as he called himself, Camille Desmarlins, was followed to execution by thousands of the kindred of those he had murdered. The wretch met his death amid the curses of the infuriated mob, and he in turn cursing them with the most vindictive hate until the fatal axe fell. A similar fate befell Sechelles, Henriot, Coffinhal, Simon, and all the leaders of the infernal Jacobin club, with perhaps two exceptions. Collot D'Herbois died in confinement and exile. Barère lived to be an old man and died universally hated, after having endured during his long life a thousand deaths from fear, disgrace, and the stings of conscience. The Girondists, who had been first to sow the storm of revolution, were the first to reap the whirlwind of destruction. Their great leaders, Vergniaud, Brissot, &c., went to the place of execution singing the revolutionary song, which they themselves, (if we mistake not,) had composed, to excite the passions of the people. Truly "did they eat of the fruits of their own ways and were filled with their own devices." And were not the horrors of the "Reign of Terror" and the dreadful sufferings entailed upon France by a war of twenty-two years with nearly all Europe, the results of the retributive justice of God? France, as a nation, had defied the power of God, and even denied his existence. As they would not have Him to reign over them, he left them to themselves, to the dominion of their own evil passions and depraved appetites. *They were just let alone, as they wished to be.* And the pathway of blood, from Moscow to the mountains of Spain, was traced by their own hands. Even the corrupt Sieyes could perceive that the punishment of Heaven was to leave his enemies to work their own will. These wretches had declared that it was their mission "to dethrone the King of Heaven, as well as the monarchs of earth." The Goddess of Reason was to be worshipped, instead of the "only wise God." Accordingly, a veiled prostitute was brought into the national assembly. One of the leaders of the municipality arose, and unveiling the figure, said, "Mortals cease to tremble before the thunders of a God whom your fears have created. Henceforth acknowledge no divinity but reason." And all France answered Amen. "The village bells were silent; Sunday was obliterated. Infancy entered the world without a blessing, and age left it without hope. In lieu of the services of the church, the fêtes of the new worship were performed by the most abandoned females; it appeared as if the Christian truth had been succeeded by the orgies of the Babylonian priests, or the grossness of the Hindoo theocracy. On every tenth day, a revolutionary leader ascended the pulpit and preached atheism to the bewildered audience; Marat was deified, and even the instrument of death sanctified by the name of the 'Holy Guillotine.' On all the public cemeteries, the inscription was placed, 'DEATH IS AN ETERNAL SLEEP.' The comedian Monort, in the church of St. Roch, carried impiety to its utmost length. 'God, if you exist,' said he, 'avenge your injured name. *I bid you defiance;* you remain silent; you dare not launch your thunders. Who after this will believe in your existence?'" (*Alison.*) God demonstrated his existence far more effectually by leaving this wretched people to work out their own ruin, than by striking the silly blasphemer dead on the spot. After one million twenty-two thousand and three hundred and fifty-one (1,022,351) victims had fallen during the Reign of Terror, a peasant standing over the dead body of the chief murderer, felt the demonstration of the Divine Being to be complete, and exclaimed, "Yes, Robespierre, there is a God." But not only was the demonstration to be written out in blood, the corollary also was to be traced in the tears of agony of the God-forsaken people. The revolutionary tribunal was overthrown, but to establish a military despotism. When Robespierre fell, Napoleon rose. France had yet to wade through blood for twenty years. Four million and one hundred and three thousand (4,103,000) of her sons were drafted for war, and their bones were scattered over every country in Europe, and even found a last resting place in Africa and Asia. And finally, a foreign army entered the capital of the nation, and imposed upon the people a sovereign whom they detested. Surely, the experiment of living without God has been tried on a sufficiently large scale, to prove that no greater curse can befall a nation than for Providence to desert those who desert him. Of all forms of retribution, this is the most terrible. The prayer of states as well as of individuals, should be, "Leave us not, neither forsake us, O God of our salvation."

We cannot close this subject without noticing the marked displeasure of God toward the inventors of instruments of torture and destruction, and also towards the devisers of horrible punishments. A cardinal invented a cage, of peculiar structure, for the punishment of heretics. He himself was confined for many years in it. Some historians relate a similar story of Tamerlane confining Bajazet, in the cage intended for the Tartar chief. The whole account is, however, discredited by others. A figure, known, as "the maiden," was devised for the punishment of Protestants. It was an image of the Virgin Mary, with extended arms. The victim was forced forward to the figure, when the arms clasped him in a deadly embrace, while hundreds of concealed lancets pierced his body. The author of this infernal device was the first to suffer by it. The guillotine takes its name from the man who contrived and perished by it. It has been said that the fatal blow that terminated the life of the Texan warrior, Col. Bowie, was from his own terrible knife. Charles II., king of Navarre, was a noted poisoner. His clothes caught fire, when saturated with brandy, and the murderous wretch had his flesh burned off to the very bones. Aaron, a courtier, recommended to the usurper Andronicus, to put out the eyes and cut off the tongues of his enemies. The cruel adviser was treated in precisely this manner, by Isaac Angelus; who dethroned and put to death Andronicus, A. D. 1203. St. Croix, a noted poisoner of the 16th century, perished by the fumes of the poisons he was making in his laboratory.

We will finish the discussion of this subject with two memorable instances of retribution. The dispersion of the Jews and the desolation of their land were foretold by Moses; and the reason assigned for the heavy judgment upon them was the neglect of the Sabbath. "Then shall the land enjoy her Sabbaths, as long as it lieth desolate, and ye be in your enemies' land; even then shall the land rest and enjoy her Sabbaths. As long as it lieth desolate shall it rest; *because it did not rest in your Sabbaths when ye dwelt upon it.*" Lev. xxvi. 34, 35. Because the Jewish people refused to observe the Sabbath, and to let their lands lie idle on God's holy day, they have been made "an astonishment, a proverb and a by-word;" and the soil, that they would not suffer to rest of their own free will, has had a long rest granted it by the sovereign will of Jehovah. Here is retribution of the most fearful kind, God vindicating the violation of his own righteous law. And this sort of retributive justice has not been confined to the Jewish nation. It has fallen upon Sabbath-breakers in every age of the world. Lord Castlereagh has not been the only violator of the sanctity of God's appointed rest, who first became a maniac and then a suicide. Sir Robert Peel, who had long observed the desecration of the Sabbath by political statesmen, &c., has given this decided testimony: "I never knew a man who habitually worked on the Sabbath, who did not fail in either mind or body."

The last instance that we will give, is one deeply engraven on the American heart. The universal verdict of the world has long since pronounced our Washington the greatest of warriors, the greatest of statesmen, and the purest of men. Macaulay closes his eulogy upon Hampden with these words: "It was when the vices and ignorance which the old tyranny had generated threatened the new freedom with destruction, that England missed that sobriety, that self-command, that perfect soundness of judgment, that perfect rectitude of intention, to which the history of revolutions furnishes no parallel, or furnishes a parallel in Washington alone." Even Byron lamented that earth had no more seed to produce a second Washington. The character of the illustrious Virginian, is reverenced in despotic Russia, as well as in free England; it is honoured equally by the haughty Spaniard as by the mercurial Frenchman. No one *now* dare question the policy or the motives of the hero, sage and Christian; but in the dark days of '76, when he and his army were enduring every privation at Valley Forge, an attempt was made to ruin his character and deprive him of his command. General Conway was the chief conspirator, and General Gates, who was to be the successor of Washington, was deeply implicated in the plot. Anonymous communications were sent to Congress, and also to Henry, then Governor of Virginia, accusing Washington of too great prudence in battle, and of incapacity to command an army. Now notice the result. Conway was compelled to resign his Inspector-General's office; he was driven into a duel with General Cadwalader, and was finally forced to hide himself to escape the indignation of the army. Gates himself showed the utmost incapacity four years after, at Camden, and such an excess of prudence, that he reached Charlotte, eighty miles distant, before any of the fugitives from his army, except a few of his personal guard. And as he had tried to supersede Washington, he himself was superseded in command of the southern army by Green, who had been true to Washington.

We have now called in sacred and profane history, and the experience of mankind to confirm the declaration of our Saviour, "For with what judgment ye judge, ye shall be judged; and with what measure ye mete, it shall be measured to you again." We have seen the bloody cut off in the midst of his days. We have seen the traitor betrayed. We have seen the slanderer of the reputation of others lose his own, and die in disgrace and infamy. We have seen the destroyer and desolater of countries himself ruined and left desolate. We have seen the tyrant oppressed, and the overthrower of dynasties himself overthrown. And we have seen the Sabbath-breaker compelled to keep a perpetual Sabbath. These instances have been collected almost at random; thousands of others might have been found in the pages of history. Gibbon, with all his scepticism, was too profound a historian, and too wise a philosopher, not to have discovered abundant traces of retributive justice in God's government of the universe. "I shall not," says he, "be readily accused of fanaticism, yet I must admit that there are often strong appearances of retribution in human affairs." Those who were even more heathenish than Gibbon himself could perceive this retribution. The myth about Tantalus perpetually tortured with hunger and thirst, for the crime of giving improper food to the gods, was but the embodiment of the universal idea, that justice in kind and degree was proportioned to the offence. And when justice was thus meted out, it met the approbation of the whole heathen world, just as it meets the approbation of all Christendom now. There is this radical difference, however, between the approval of the true Christian and that of the followers of false creeds; the Christian only approves when God or his appointed delegates measure out the punishment. The heathen have ever claimed the right to retaliate wrong themselves. In the one case it is retributive justice, in the other it is vengeance.

HYPOCRISY AND CENSORIOUSNESS.

"Thou hypocrite, first cast out the beam out of thine own eye, and then shalt thou see clearly to cast out the mote out of thy brother's eye." (Ver. 8.)

Here the pretender to sanctity, and the fault-finder, are placed in the same category; they constitute one and the same person. The reason of the identity is plain. The meek and lowly Jesus is the corner-stone of the temple of holiness. Humility is the root of the tree of righteousness; and the deeper the root strikes down into the soil of abasement, the lovelier will the fruits of the Spirit hang from the boughs. And among the golden clusters will be love, long-suffering, gentleness, goodness, meekness. Gal. v. 22. Pride is a plant of different growth. Its baneful root is in the summit of inflation, and its noxious fruits are hatred, variance, emulation, wrath, strife. Gal. v. 20. The disciple of the gentle Redeemer cannot, then, delight in censure. The proud child of Satan cannot, then, delight in praise. He who is adorned with the graces of the Spirit, is too meek to be a reprover. He who is endued with the temper and disposition of the Prince of Darkness, is an "accuser," like his master. He to whom the Spirit of Truth has shown the corruption of his own heart, is too much self-abased to be intolerant of the sins of others. He whom the father of lies has inflated with self-conceit and self-righteousness, is prone to judge harshly, and to persecute bitterly. And thus a censorious spirit is a good test of hypocrisy and the unregenerate state. Old Thomas Fuller has justly said: "Now by these shrewd signs a dissembler is often discovered. First: Heavy censuring of others for light faults. Second: Boasting of his own goodness, &c." And the author of "Self-Knowledge" has in like manner pointed out the connection between hypocrisy and censoriousness. Mason, commenting on the 3d, 4th and 5th verses of this chapter, says, "Four things are intimated: First—That some are much more quicksighted to discern the faults of others than their own. Second—That they are often the most forward to correct and cure the foibles of others, who are least qualified for that office. Third—That they who are inclined to deal in censure should always begin at home. Fourth—*Great censoriousness is great hypocrisy.*

"This common failing of human nature the heathen were very sensible of, and imaged it in the following manner. Every man, say they, carries two bags with him; the one hanging before him and the other behind him; into that before, he puts the faults of others; into that behind, his own. By which means he never sees his own failings, whilst he has those of others always before his eyes." (*John Mason.*)

It was a saying of Socrates, (as reported by Cicero,) that the easiest way for the hypocrite to be popular, was to practise the virtues which he pretended to have. *He* thinks differently, however, and hopes to build his reputation upon the ruin of that of others. He seeks to dim the lustre of the character of his neighbour, that his own may shine out by contrast. If there were no eagles, carrion crows might be esteemed noble birds. If there were no virtuous men, the obscene feeders on the characters of others might be esteemed pure and holy. The fault-finding hypocrite does not strive "to lift a mortal to the skies," but "to pull an angel down." He does not aim to excel others in goodness and truth, but to bring them down to his own level, or to sink them beneath him.

To sum up the whole matter, then, censoriousness results from three things; 1st. Pride; the truly humble sees too plainly the beam in his own eye, to be troubled about the mote in his brother's. 2d. Uncharitableness; "Charity thinketh no evil." The censorious is destitute of that grace, without which all other attainments are "but as sounding brass and a tinkling cymbal." 3d. Envy; the censorious is uneasy, mortified and discontented, on account of the real or supposed excellencies of his neighbour, and endeavours to degrade him. Censoriousness proceeds from one of these sources, or from all three combined. It is a foul blot upon the Church, but is by no means confined to it. Those who delight in hunting out the failings of the professed disciples of Jesus Christ, and then triumphantly plume themselves on not being hypocrites, are, of all men in the world, fault-finding hypocrites. What but a spirit of envy and detraction makes them find pleasure in the corruption of the Church? What but a desire to bring others down to their own degraded level? And yet they look with great complacency upon the sins of Christians, and in the pride of their hearts are ready to thank God that they are not hypocrites; apparently unconscious that the vilest form of hypocrisy is that which seeks to exalt itself by the overthrow of another. No animals are so detested and detestable as those which fatten themselves on corruption.

IMPROPER SUBJECTS OF REPROOF.

"Give not that which is holy unto the dogs, neither cast ye your pearls before swine, lest they trample them under their feet and turn again and rend you." (Ver. 6.)

This verse furnishes an instance of what is called the *introverted parallelism;* that is, where the first and fourth lines of the verse correspond, and the second corresponds with the third. We might write it thus:

> Give not that which is holy unto the dogs,
> Neither cast ye your pearls before swine,
> Lest they trample them under their feet,
> And turn again (i. e. the dogs) and rend you.
> (*Barnes' Notes on the Gospels.*)

The connection between this verse and the five preceding verses, is apparent. We had there the qualifications of reprovers, here of the reproved. Scott justly says, "As every man is not qualified or authorized to be a reprover, so every offender is not the proper subject of reproof. To persevere in giving instruction or counsel to some men, would be as improper as to throw the holy things, which were the food of the priests, unto unclean dogs; or to cast pearls before swine." Two classes of persons are represented in the sixth verse to be improper subjects of reproof. We may in plain language designate the first as the dog class; and the second as the hog class. The dog stands as the type of the snarling, snapping sneerer and scorner. The hog is the fit emblem of the filthy and foolish, the lewd and the licentious. The growling cynic, Voltaire, furnishes a fine specimen of the canine class, while the low, drunken debauchee, Tom Paine, stands out preëminently as the representative of the swine class, wallowing in the mire, and glorying in their shame. Both dogs and swine were unclean in the Mosaic economy, and were regarded with abhorrence by the Jews. The word *dog* was the strongest possible epithet of contempt. "Is thy servant a dog, that he should do this great thing?" said the indignant Hazael, when foretold the enormities that he would commit. And David, to show Saul that he was disgracing himself by his unjust persecution of an innocent man, used the following language: "After whom is the king of Israel come out? After whom dost thou pursue? after a dead dog?" In regard to swine, the Jews held them in such detestation, that it is said they would not even name them. The servants of Antiochus Epiphanes attempted to force swine's flesh into the mouth of Eleazar; but he suffered death rather than swallow the abomination. It is evident, then, from the employment of such strong epithets to designate the scoffer and the impure, that they are an abomination in the eyes of the Lord. The disciples are directed not to waste the precious truths of the gospel upon them. "It is not meet to take the children's bread and cast it to the dogs." Instead of feeding upon it thankfully, they will turn again and rend the giver. The wisest of men said, "Reprove not a scorner, lest he hate thee." "A scorner loveth not one that reproveth him." "He that reproveth a scorner, getteth to himself shame; and he that rebuketh a wicked man, getteth himself a blot." And we have also given us the reason of the desperate condition of the scoffer and blasphemer. It is found in this, that God metes out to him the same measure with which he measures. "Surely he *scorneth the scorner;* but he giveth grace unto the lowly." As the scorner has put away the fear of the Lord, the only true source of wisdom, he cannot be made wise or amended by reproof. Therefore it is idle to admonish him. "A scorner seeketh wisdom and findeth it not." Deserted by God, groping along in his sin-darkened condition, he is still too proud to listen to the voice of warning and reproof. "A scorner heareth not rebuke." It is folly to censure a deaf man. The ribald jester at divine truth, the bold blasphemer, is not a proper subject of reproof.

Neither are the lewd proper subjects of reproof. The object of Christian rebuke is to affect the conscience by convincing the understanding. But Solomon says of the impure that they "lack understanding," Prov. vi. 32. They are fools, and "fools make a mock at sin." It is unseemly to admonish them; "for excellent speech becometh not a fool." He glories in his shame: "it is abomination for a fool to depart from evil." The hog is his faithful representative, and as it will not give up the mire and the mud-puddle, so he will not give up his filth and beastliness. "Having eyes full of adultery and *that cannot cease from sin.*" It is doubtless the duty of the gospel ministry to rebuke every species of sin. He that rides upon the white horse with his crown and bow, may barb his arrow with the truth so proclaimed, and send it home to the heart of the scoffer and the adulterer. But we think that private individuals are plainly forbidden to reprove the reviler and the dissolute. "Reproofs of instruction are ill-bestowed upon such, and expose the reprover to all the contempt and mischief that might be expected from dogs and swine. One can expect no other than that they will trample the reproofs under their feet, in scorn of them and rage against them; for they are impatient of control and contradiction; and they will turn again and rend the reprovers: rend their good name with their revilings, return them wounding words for their healing ones; rend them with persecution, as Herod did John the Baptist for his faithfulness." (*Matthew Henry.*) And here we would remark, that when we look upon the limitations thrown around the exercise of reproving, there should be but little of it; 1st. In regard to those who reprove, since none but the delegates of God can claim the privilege, and that only in their official capacity: 2d. In regard to the reproved, how large a portion of mankind belong to the two classes, which are exempt from rebuke because of the vileness of their characters. It seems that with these restrictions, reproving must be confined chiefly to Christians themselves. The erring brother may be "restored" not slandered, not reviled, and it must be done only by the "*spiritual,*" and "*in the spirit of meekness.*" If a brother wrong us, we may *tell* him of his fault privately, not *reprove* him for it, still less reprove him publicly. If he will not hear us, we may take with us one or two more to establish the truth of our statement. And if he still remain obdurate, we may then refer the matter to the church, the delegate of God. Matt. xviii.

ENCOURAGEMENTS TO PRAYER.

"Ask, and it shall be given you; seek, and ye shall find; knock, and it shall be opened unto you. For every one that asketh receiveth; and he that seeketh findeth; and to him that knocketh it shall be opened." (Verses 7, 8.)

Asking implies want. We are "wretched and miserable, and poor and blind and naked." We need "gold tried in the fire," even enduring riches that will last when the world is in flames; we need "the white raiment" of Jesus' perfect righteousness, that "the shame of our nakedness do not appear;" we need the anointing of the Spirit, that we "may see" things in their true value, in the light of eternity. We want pardon, we want joy in the Holy Ghost, we want sanctification of the Spirit.

Seeking implies loss. We have lost the favour of God, we have lost our title to heaven, we have lost the approbation of a good conscience.

Knocking implies an earnest desire to find shelter within the sanctuary of mercy, from the fury of the storm without. The cloud that drives to this refuge, however black it may seem, is still the messenger of a God of mercy.

But there is far more implied in these three imperatives, than all this. The primary signification, as we understand it, is, ask imploringly for the way of life, diligently seek it, and knock earnestly at the door, even Christ Jesus, that leads into it. And the promise annexed is, that the inquirer shall receive the necessary information; the diligent seeker shall find it; and the earnest knocker shall be admitted into it. The first act of the awakened sinner is one of inquiry. "Men and brethren, what shall we do?" was the anxious inquiry of the three thousand, who were pricked to the heart on the day of Pentecost. "Lord, what wilt thou have me to do," asked poor Saul in his amazement and distress, as he lay stretched on the ground, with the bright light shining about him.

"Sirs, what must I do to be saved?" inquired the trembling jailer of Paul and Silas. Bunyan, in his inimitable allegory, has most happily explained the meaning of asking, seeking, and knocking. He saw in his dream, the man clothed in rags, with the great burden on his back, "looking this way and that way as if he would run, yet he stood still, because he could not tell which way to go." And he heard this distressed man crying "what shall I do?" Then Evangelist came to him and asked him, "why standest thou still?" He answered, "because I know not whither to go." Upon this, Evangelist "gave him a parchment roll; and there was written within, 'flee from the wrath to come.' The man therefore read it, and looking upon it very carefully, said, 'whither must I flee?' Then said Evangelist, pointing with his finger over a very wide field, 'do you see yonder wicket-gate?' He said, 'No.' Then said the other, 'do you see yonder shining light?' He said, 'I think I do.' Then said Evangelist, 'Keep that light in your eye, and go up directly thereto, so shalt thou see the gate; at which, when thou knockest, it shall be told thee what to do.' So I saw in my dream, that the man began to run. . . . . So in process of time, Christian got up to the gate. Now over the gate was written, 'Knock, and it shall be opened unto you.'" Here we have the inquiry, the seeking, and the knocking. The wicket-gate represents the Redeemer. He says of himself, "I am the door: by me, if any man enter in, he shall be saved, and shall go in and out, and find pasture," John x. 9. And Paul, speaking of him, says: "For *through him* we both have access by one Spirit unto the Father," Ephes. ii. 18. "He that entereth not by the door into the sheep-fold, but climbeth up some other way, the same is a thief and a robber." There is no access to God, but by Jesus Christ. To all, who have not passed through this door of hope, the dreadful Jehovah is and must be, a consuming fire. What loveliness can his pure and holy eyes see in a sin-polluted wretch? "How should man be just with God? If he will contend with him, he cannot answer him one of a thousand." If "our righteousnesses are but filthy rags" in his sight, how must our sins and abominations appear!

But all who enter into the sheep-fold by the door, are safe from the fierce indignation of an offended God. They belong to the "Good Shepherd, who giveth his life for the sheep," and the "Father himself loveth them," because of his love for the Good Shepherd.

Our Saviour then employs these three imperatives, because they express the highest office of prayer: the taking up of the sinner in his rags and filth with the great burden on his back, pointing him to the open door, helping him to seek it by the light of God's truth, and enabling him to knock at it, and go in and sup with the Lord of the mansion. However, as the address is to disciples, there is a subordinate sense, in which, ask, seek, and knock is used, and one in harmony with the preceding verses. With the sixth verse ends all that is said, directly, of the practical errors of the Scribes and Pharisees. Our Saviour had exposed the errors, which these sects taught with their lips and exemplified in their lives. He had shown their religion to be hollow, formal, hypocritical, devoid of life-giving power and energy. He had declared that the religion of his followers must far exceed theirs; it must be sincere, earnest, embracing the inner worship of the heart, forbidding every angry emotion, every impure thought, every improper word, every worldly desire, every ostentatious act, every harsh opinion, every malevolent wish. We can imagine that the hearts of the disciples sank more and more within them, as their Master unfolded his moral system, in all its severe beauty, unbending integrity, and matchless purity; until they were ready to exclaim, "Lord, we are of unclean lips, and dwell in the midst of a people of unclean lips, and thou requirest of us the holiness of angels around the throne." When thus shut up to feel their utter helplessness, their entire inability to comply with the requisitions of this perfect code, they are then shown that their "sufficiency must be of God;" that his strength is made perfect in their weakness, and their weakness made perfect in his strength. They are taught to ask, to seek, and to knock for the grace that shall be sufficient for them. And the word of a God of truth is pledged, that the effort shall not be in vain. "For every one that asketh, receiveth; and he that seeketh, findeth; and to him that knocketh, it shall be opened." The repetition of the promise in the 8th verse gives, as it were, a double guaranty on the part of God, that believing prayer shall not be offered in vain. So that if we do not come up to the high standard of duty prescribed, we are left wholly without excuse. We fail in duty, simply because we fail in prayer. God has promised all needed grace, if we perform all needed prayer. The absence of sufficient grace proves then the absence of sufficient prayer. It is no answer, to say that no mere man has ever been free of malevolence, carnal emotions, worldly-mindedness, uncharitable thoughts, &c. That is true, but are we excusable because we are sinful? Is our want of freedom from corruption the result of God's unfaithfulness to his promise of hearing prayer, or of our unfaithfulness in prayer? Let God be true and every man a liar. The fault is in ourselves, and that we may be the better able to see exactly where it lies, we will examine the next three verses, which not only contain encouragement to prayer, but also most beautifully explain the spirit and nature of prayer.

"Or what man is there of you, whom if his son ask bread, will he give him a stone? Or if he ask a fish, will he give him a serpent? If ye then being evil know how to give good gifts unto your children, how much more shall your Father which is in heaven give good things to them that ask him?" (Verses 9–11.)

Prayer is here likened to the asking for food, by

children of a tender parent. This expresses exactly its nature and spirit. In its nature, it is simply an asking, not an eloquent address, and may be expressed as effectually by a look, as by the most elaborate appeal. Its spirit must be that of a child asking for food. Want must prompt the petition, humility must clothe it, and a child-like confidence must be felt that it will be heard. These are the three elements that make the asking of the child effectual; these are the three elements that make prayer to God effectual. The pleading of want, humility, and faith was never made in vain. An evil parent cannot resist them in his child. A holy God will not resist them in his creature. He may not answer the prayer in the way that the creature expected, but he will answer it in a better way. The parent may not give his hungry child exactly the kind of food that he asks for, but he will not give him a useless stone, still less will he give him a noxious serpent. In his superior wisdom, the parent may see that the food craved is not healthy, is not suitable for his son. He will not leave his child to the pangs of hunger, but he will "feed him with food convenient for him." He will give him that which is more nourishing and more appropriate. And thus it is with God. He may not answer the humble, child-like prayer, in the manner prayed for, but he has not turned a deaf ear to it. In our sin-blinded condition we cannot pray, we cannot even "order our conversation aright by reason of darkness." What we greatly desire, as a blessing, might prove a fearful curse. And what we most dread, may prove a great blessing. "For who knoweth what is good for man in this life, all the days of his vain life, which he spendeth as a shadow?" Let us then perform the duty of prayer, and leave the mode of its answer, entirely, to the only wise God. He did not answer Paul, when he besought him thrice to take away the thorn in the flesh. The thorn was needful to keep Paul from self-elation, at the abundance of his revelations. He was not answered in his own way, but he *was* answered in God's way, which was infinitely better. And so Paul felt and exclaimed, when he perceived God's better way, "Therefore will I glory in my infirmities." The Lord did not answer the prayer of Moses, when he asked to be blotted out of God's book, if the Israelites were blotted out. He was not answered according to his folly, for it would have been inconsistent with the justice of God to grant his request. "And the Lord said unto Moses, Whosoever hath sinned against me, him will I blot out of my book. Therefore now go, lead the people unto the place of which I have spoken unto thee: behold, mine angel shall go before thee: nevertheless, in the day when I visit, I will visit their sin upon them." Exod. xxxii. 33, 34. The answer that Moses received was infinitely better than what he sought. It was consistent with the justice of God, full of mercy to himself and of encouragement to persevere in the path of duty. The promise to Moses is similar to that to Paul. The

Angel of the Covenant was to sustain the one, and the grace of the Lord, the other. David was not answered in his own way, when he asked for the life of his child. But the refusal heightened his conviction of sin, showed him the enormity of the act that he had committed, and it is probable, prompted that penitential psalm, which has brought thousands and tens of thousands to the feet of Jesus. The prayer was answered in God's better way, and so David doubtless felt when he said: "It is good for me that I have been afflicted."

Many a parent, like David, has poured out his soul in agony unutterable for the life of his child, and yet death came. It may be that the child, if spared, would have dishonoured God and ruined his own soul. It may be that the parent himself needed the punishment; needed to be pruned, that he might bear more fruit. It may be that love for the child concealed and covered up the love for God. It was necessary, then, to remove the creature that the Creator might be all in all. The lamps in the hands of Gideon's warriors did not shine out until the pitchers were broken, and the trumpets were sounding for battle. The light of Christian character is often obscured, until the frail earthen vase that conceals it is shivered to pieces, and God sounds the signal for conflict with sorrow and anguish.

Let us, then, learn to let God answer our prayers in his own way, assured that that way is best for his own glory and our happiness. And so all our prayers that relate to mere temporal well-being should be conditional. "Father, if it be thy will, let this cup of suffering pass; nevertheless, not my will, but thine be done." "Father, if it be thy will, grant me this blessing; nevertheless, not my will, but thine be done." Hezekiah prayed unconditionally for life. This prayer was granted, and he lived to dishonour God, and bring ruin on his family and nation. The king of Babylon sent messengers to *congratulate him on his recovery from sickness*, and in the pride of his heart he showed them all his treasures. And then Isaiah came unto him, with a message from the Lord. "Behold, the days come, that all that is in thine house, and that which thy fathers have laid up in store until this day, shall be carried to Babylon; nothing shall be left, saith the Lord. And of thy sons that shall issue from thee, which thou shalt beget, shall they take away; and they shall be eunuchs in the palace of the king of Babylon." Isa. xxxix. 6, 7. Here the connection is obvious, between the answer to his prayer and his sin, with its subsequent punishment. The lesson thus taught, should be remembered by all, and supposed blessings be prayed for, if consistent with God's glory and our highest interests. Things which are not revealed to us as the proper objects of prayer, should never be prayed for, without annexing the condition, that His will, and not ours, be done. Life, health, reputation, property, children, friends, all temporal things, should be committed unto Him as unto a faithful Creator. Prayer, in reference to these objects, should always be conditional. But as St. Luke explains "the good things," spoken of in the 11th verse, to be the gift of the Spirit, (Luke xi. 13,) we may ask unconditionally for His holy influences. God is ever more ready to grant his Spirit than we are to ask honestly and sincerely for his blessed presence. The prayer for the Spirit cannot be offered too often, too importunately, and too earnestly; nor yet too absolutely and unconditionally. It is the work of that holy Being to draw us to Christ, and enable us to close in with the offer of salvation. It is his work to change the heart, to renew the will, to sanctify our affections, and fit us for a residence with God and holy beings. All acceptable prayer must be dictated by him. The very first breathing of the soul should be for his sanctifying influences, that the petition may be aright. The earth lay without form, a dark chaotic void, until the Spirit of God moved upon the waters. All right desires lie hidden in the soul—crude, shapeless, dead—until the Spirit brood over them and give them figure, life and activity. The Spirit alone can make the man, dead in trespasses and sins, alive in Christ Jesus. The slain, in the valley of dry bones, could not live, until the breath came from the four winds to breathe upon them. Ezek. xxxvii. 9. Though Christ has been offered up as a sacrifice for sin, no man ever yet was willing to receive him as a Saviour, until drawn unto him by the third person of the Holy Trinity. Nor would the pleadings of any man ever find favour with a

Holy God, but for the intercession of the Spirit, "with groanings that cannot be uttered."

How cheering and comforting it is to know that God is more ready to send this renewing, sanctifying, interceding Spirit, than parents are to give good things to their children. Here is the great encouragement to prayer—the promise of the Spirit. We are dark, ignorant, short-sighted, and know not how to frame our petitions aright. He has all wisdom, and will enlighten our understandings. Our hearts are cold and dead, but he will give them warmth and life. God, because of our sins, "has covered himself with a thick cloud, that our prayer should not pass through." But when his Spirit has enabled us to believe on his Son, he will say: "I have blotted out, as a thick cloud, thy transgressions, and as a cloud, thy sins; return unto me, for I have redeemed thee." Our "prayer will then be unto thee, O Lord, in an acceptable time;" "and God, even our own God, shall bless us."

Our confidence, then, in the answer to prayer for right things, and offered in the right manner, may be drawn from this promise of the Spirit. The greater gift includes the smaller. If God will send the Sanctifier and Comforter to renew and purify, to cheer and console, how much more will he give all needed blessings of an inferior nature to those who ask in the name of Christ. "Ye have not chosen me, but I have chosen you, and ordained you, that ye should go and bring forth fruit, and that your fruit should remain;

that *whatsoever* ye shall ask of the Father in my name, he may give it." Our blessed Redeemer had first promised the Comforter, and then the inferior blessing of granting *whatsoever* was asked in his name. The reason for the promise is given in the very words which convey it, "That ye may go and bring forth fruit." This is the great end of the promise. The Spirit is given in order that God may be glorified by the good works of his sanctified children. Here, then, we have full, complete encouragement to prayer, resting first on the promise of the Spirit; and that again resting upon God's desire for his own glory. Nothing more can be added to this—nothing more is needed.

We will next consider some species of so called prayer, which are not acceptable, and which are therefore not answered.

UNANSWERED PRAYER.

Of this sort of prayer we make the following classification.

1st. Uncandid Prayer. "If I regard iniquity in my heart, the Lord will not hear me," said the inspired Psalmist. God will not be mocked. It is in vain to ask him for a clean heart and a renewed will, if we ask with the secret purpose of continuing in known sin. We are but attempting to deceive the Searcher of hearts and Trier of the reins. He "understands our thoughts afar off," and "there is not a word in our tongues, but lo, O Lord, thou knowest it altogether." Hollow professions do not often deceive men; but they excite the wrath of Him, who "knoweth us altogether." He will not answer the prayer for personal holiness, where there is the unavowed intention in the heart to cling to some darling sin. To pray for the advance of Christ's kingdom, and then to bring reproach upon his name by an unholy life, is to play the part of Judas. It is betraying our Master with a kiss of professed friendship and love. But to pray, for the advance of his kingdom with secret hatred in our hearts to his rule and dominion, is to play the part of the bloody wretches, who in Pilate's hall arrayed him in the semblance of royal robes, put a crown of thorns on his head and a reed-sceptre in his hand; all in mockery and scorn. Father in Heaven, "cleanse thou us from secret faults," that we may not thus insult thee and mock thy Son. And as thou wouldest not accept from thine own people a sacrifice with any blemish upon it, we pray that thy Spirit may enable us to offer a pure offering, a heart untainted by any cherished sin.

"A cherished corruption in the mind is the more likely to interpose between God and the soul, because it does not assume the shape and bulk of crime. A practical offence, the sudden effect of temptation, is more likely to be followed by keen repentance, deep self-abasement, and fervent application for pardon; whereas to the close bosom-sin, knowing that no human charge can be brought against it, the soul secretly returns with a fondness facilitated by long indulgence." (*Hannah More.*) The whole drift of the 58th chapter of Isaiah is, that he who would offer acceptable prayer, must give up indulgence of known sin. "Ye shall not offer unto the Lord," said Moses, "that which is bruised, or crushed, or broken or cut." He will not have the oblation of a heart all scarred and disfigured by sin.

But God not only will not listen to the prayer that the body may be made the temple of the Holy Ghost, when the unacknowledged resolution of the soul is to pollute and defile that temple by sin; he not only does not listen to such prayer, he regards it with abhorrence. "The sacrifice of the wicked is an abomination to the Lord." Isaiah, in speaking of the assembly for prayer of those who still cling to their corruptions, says, "it is iniquity, even the solemn meeting." Hosea goes still farther, and teaches that vain offerings will but cause God to remember the iniquities of the offerers. "They sacrifice flesh for the sacrifices of mine offerings, and eat it; but the Lord accepteth them not; *now* will he remember their iniquity and visit their sins." When an enemy approaches us with specious flattery, we are prone to recall his former acts of hostility. And thus it is with God; the uncandid prayer—the prayer with the lips for holiness, while the heart resolves to cling to some cherished lust—but serves to remind Him of the disobedience and rebellion of the supplicant.

2d. Prayer for improper things.

"Ye ask and receive not," says James, "because

ye ask amiss, that ye may consume it upon your lusts." Prayer for calamity upon enemies; prayer for worldly power and riches, to be used against the glory of God and advancement of Christ's kingdom; prayer for objects to gratify pride, ambition, revenge, and all unholy feelings, will not be heard. It is asking amiss, to consume upon worldly lusts.

Prayer for improper things may be offered both by the children of God and by the ungodly. When presented by the former, God may reject it, consistently with his promise to be a prayer-hearing God. No wise parent would grant to the importunity of his child that which would do him harm. When presented by the wicked, the prayer is the preposterous demand of an insolent and unworthy beggar.

The Scriptures give us some examples of prayers that were not granted, because the things asked for were improper. Moses greatly desired to be permitted to enter the promised land, and besought this favour of the Lord. But God intended the punishment of Moses to be a warning to his people for all time, and therefore replied to his prayer: "Let it suffice thee; speak no more unto me of this matter. Get thee up into the top of Pisgah, and lift up thine eyes westward, and northward, and southward, and eastward, and behold it with thine eyes; for thou shalt not go over this Jordan." Deut. iii. 26, 27. Jonah prayed unto God for death. But it was the prayer of petulance, impatience and mortified pride, and the Lord did not hear him. No child of God has a right to pray for death, because of the trials and difficulties that surround him. The Creator may use his creature as a buoy on a tempest-tost sea, to warn others of rocks and quicksands; and the creature has no right to complain of the beating of the storm and the swelling of the waves. Elijah, in his despondency, as he sat under the juniper-tree in the wilderness, said, "It is enough, now, O Lord, take away my life, for I am not better than my fathers." But God did not hear his prayer. The servant still had a great work to do. He had yet to anoint Hazael king of Syria, Jehu to be king over Israel, and Elisha to be a prophet in his room. 1 Kings xix. 15, 16. He had yet to carry the message of God's vengeance to Ahab and Jezebel, for the murder of Naboth the Jezreelite; he had yet to rebuke king Ahaziah, for inquiring of Baal-zebub instead of the Lord; he had yet to vindicate the majesty of Heaven, by the calling down fire from heaven upon the two captains of Ahaziah, with their companies of fifty; and finally, instead of leaving his body in the wilderness, a prey to beasts and birds, he had yet to ascend in a chariot of fire to the God whom he had served.

The disciples, James and John, were not heard, when they asked their Master to be placed, the one on the right hand and the other on the left, in his glory. It was an ambitious petition—a request for worldly distinction; and our Saviour taught them that they who would be great among them, must be their servant. And when these same disciples prayed for permission to bring down fire from heaven upon a village of the Samaritans, they met with a stern rebuke instead of an answer to their request. "But he turned and rebuked them, and said, Ye know not what manner of spirit ye are of; for the Son of Man is not come to destroy men's lives, but to save them."

3d. Spasmodic prayer.

The irregular, fitful devotion that manifests itself only in seasons of alarm, distress or calamity, has no claim upon an answer from God: "But ye have set at naught all my counsel, and would none of my reproof: I also will laugh at your calamity; I will mock when your fear cometh." Prov. i. 25, 26. "Therefore it is come to pass, that, as he cried, and they would not hear; so they cried, and I would not hear, saith the Lord of hosts." Zech. vii. 13. "Thus saith the Lord unto this people, Thus have they loved to wander, they have not refrained their feet; therefore the Lord doth not accept them. When they fast, I will not hear their cry." Jer. xiv. 10–12. "They are turned back to the iniquities of their forefathers, which refused to hear my words . . . . . therefore, thus saith the Lord, Behold, I will bring evil upon them, which they shall not be able to escape; and though they shall cry unto me, I will not hearken unto them." Jer. xi. 10–12.

God is surely under no sort of obligation to attend to the cry of those who only approach him when in trouble. He *may* hear them out of the abundance of his mercy and compassion, but not because of the obligation of his promise to hear prayer. The most tender parent may refuse a boon to a child, who only shows affection when he wants to use his father as a convenience.

This spasmodic prayer is in direct conflict with the teachings of God's holy word. He will have his children to cultivate a spirit of habitual prayer. "Watch ye, therefore, and *pray always*, that ye may be accounted worthy to escape all those things that shall come to pass." Luke xxi. 36. "Continuing instant in prayer." Rom. xii. 12. "Be careful for nothing; but *in every thing*, by prayer and supplication, with thanksgiving, let your requests be made known unto God." Phil. iv. 6. "*Pray without ceasing*." 1 Thess. v. 17. "Night and day, praying exceedingly." 1 Thess. iii. 10. "And he spake a parable unto them to this end, that men ought *always* to pray, and not to faint." Luke xviii. 1. David could say, "Seven times a day do I praise thee, because of thy righteous judgments." Seven was a perfect number with the Hebrews, and is often taken to signify an infinite quantity. The Psalmist most probably meant that he was ever in a praying frame of mind. This is just the spirit to be cultivated by every sincere Christian. Under the Mosaic dispensation, the fire which descended from heaven at the dedication of the tabernacle, was sacredly preserved and never suffered to go out. In like manner, the flame of devotion should never be allowed to flicker and grow dim in the heart of the true disciple of the Lord Jesus.

4th. Prayer without faith.

"All things whatsoever," said our Saviour, "ye shall ask in prayer, *believing*, ye shall receive." Again: "What things soever ye desire when ye pray, *believe* that ye receive them, and ye shall have them." Mark xi. 24. Again: "If ye had faith as a grain of mustard seed, ye might say unto this sycamine-tree, be thou plucked up by the root, and be thou planted in the sea, and it should obey you." Luke xvii. 6. Such are the promises to the prayer of faith; and the fulness of the answer is ever measured by the proportion of faith in the offerer of the prayer. "Go thy way, and *as thou hast believed, so be it done unto thee.*" Matt. viii. 13. "Daughter, be of good comfort; thy faith has made thee whole." Matt. ix. 22. "Be not afraid, only believe," was the language to the poor bereaved ruler of the synagogue. When the father brought the child afflicted with the dumb spirit, "Jesus said unto him, If thou canst believe, all things are possible to him that believeth." Mark ix. 23. The persevering, believing woman of Canaan, was commended thus: "O woman, great is thy faith; be it unto thee even as thou wilt." Matt. xv. 28. The two blind men were to be wholly or partially restored to sight, or not restoredat all, according as they fully or partially believed, or utterly disbelieved. "Then touched he their eyes, saying, According to your faith be it unto you." Matt. ix. 29. "If any of you lack wisdom," says James, "let him ask of God, and it shall be given him. But let him ask in faith, nothing wavering; for he that wavereth, is like a wave of the sea driven with the wind and tossed. For *let not that man think that he shall receive any thing of the Lord.*" James i. 6, 7. John explains the ground of faith in prayer, and at the same time the proper objects of faith: "And this is the confidence that we have in him, that if we ask any thing according to his will, he heareth us; and if we know that he hear us, whatsoever we ask, we know that we have the petitions that we desired of him." 1 John v. 14, 15. The promise of God constitutes, then, the ground of faith; and the things promised are those upon which faith can most surely be exercised. David made God's promise to establish his house, a motive to plead with God to do as he had said. 2 Sam. vii. 16–25. God had said, "I will send rain upon the earth;" yet Elijah must pray, and with great earnestness and perseverance, too, for what God had promised. 1 Kings xviii. 42–44. When Daniel knew that the seventy years of captivity were expiring, then he set his face to seek by prayers the promised deliverance. Dan. ix. 2, 3. When our Lord had promised the gift of the Holy Spirit, the disciples continued in prayer and supplication till the fulfilment of the promise. Acts i. 14. (*Mine Explored.*) If Christians of the present day would but exercise the same faith in the promise, that "The kingdoms of this world are to become the kingdoms of our Lord and of his Christ;" and if they would but offer earnest, persevering prayer for its fulfilment, the Spirit of God would be poured out yet more abundantly upon our land and the whole earth. God's arm is not shortened, but limitations are continually put upon the exercise of his gracious power by the weakness of faith of his own people. They can pray with some sort of confidence for the conversion of a few; but their belief is not strong enough to embrace great multitudes. Even Moses, who had witnessed so many mighty wonders at the hands of God, could not believe that the Omnipotent could feed six hundred thousand footmen with flesh for a whole month. "Shall the flocks and herds be slain for them, to suffice them? or shall the fish of the sea be gathered together for them, to suffice them? And the Lord said unto Moses, Is the Lord's hand waxed short? thou shalt see now whether my word shall come to pass unto thee or not." If the faith of God's people were but strong enough and enlarged enough, more than six hundred thousand would be fed with "bread from heaven;" more than six hundred thousand would be fed with that "flesh" which "is meat, indeed." May the Redeemer grant his followers more faith, so that they may not be obstacles in the way of the chariots of salvation.

CRITICAL EXAMINATION.

A more minute inspection of the first eleven verses of the seventh chapter, may be profitable. The word rendered "judge" in the first verse, is often used in the sense of condemn. (*Olshausen.*) This is obviously the meaning here, since in the parallel passage, Luke vi. 37, we have "judge not and ye shall not be judged, condemn not and ye shall not be condemned." The apposition of the words "judge" and "condemn," shows that unfavourable judgment is meant. And here we would remark, that the verse in Luke affords no comfort to moralists, who think that their professed charity and universal toleration of all creeds and sects constitute a sure hope of salvation. Do these pseudo-philanthropists *judge* favourably of Christ and the claims of his gospel? Are they willing to "have this man rule over them?" If they reject his easy reign and judge him harshly, can they complain of being rejected by him and condemned in the great day of Judgment?

The word rendered "mote" in the 3d, 4th and 5th verses, may also be rendered *splinter*, *paring* or *peeling*. The splinter from the beam is in contrast with the whole beam.

In the 8th verse, we have a remarkable transition from the present tense to the second future passive. "Every one asking, receiveth, and seeking, findeth, and knocking, *shall* have it opened unto him." There is no promise here of an instantaneous opening of the door of mercy. This delay in accepting the sinner may be to try his faith, as in the case of the Syrophenician woman; or to test his sincerity, as in the case of the Scribe, who said, "Master, I will follow thee, whithersoever thou goest." But whatever the reason may be, the fact is certain that many are kept waiting long at the very threshold, and alas! many like the rich young man, whom Jesus loved, turn away sorrowing, when "not far from the kingdom of God."

In the 11th verse, the word rendered "heaven" is in the plural. The God of the universe, and not the believer's Father, is, as we understand it, the Being here alluded to. If so, the "ye" refers to the natural and not to the renewed condition of the disciples. The universal depravity of man is not taught as something new, but recognized as an acknowledged truth. "*All* we, like sheep, have gone astray; we have turned *every one* to his own way; and the Lord hath laid on him the iniquity of us *all.*" "I have gone astray, like a lost sheep," said the man after God's own heart. "There is none righteous, no, not one. There is none that understandeth, there is none that seeketh after God." But the "being evil" may justly apply to regenerate men. Every child of God, who knows his own heart, must feel with good Bishop Beveridge, that his "very tears of repentance need to be washed in the blood of Christ." The Bible gives us an account of but one sinless man—the man of Calvary. And it is remarkable, that it tells us of holy men committing those very sins and follies which they seemed least likely to commit. Moses, who was "very meek above all the men which were upon the face of the earth," became very angry and "spake unadvisedly with his lips." We have all heard of the "patience of Job," and also of his petulance and fretfulness. The pure-hearted David committed adultery. Solomon "passed all the kings of the earth in riches and wisdom," yet even he became foolish and "and loved many strange women." The gentle, loving and lovable John, on a certain occasion, showed the most vindictive hate against a village of the Samaritans, and wished to call down fire from heaven to consume it. The bold, sturdy Peter trembled before a servant-maid, and lied in his fright, to escape from an imaginary danger. Paul was humble enough to call himself the chief of sinners, and "least of all the apostles, not meet to be called an apostle," "less than the least of all saints;" and yet Paul had given to him, "a thorn in the flesh, the messenger of Satan to buffet him," lest he should be filled with pride and self-conceit.

THE GOLDEN RULE.

"Therefore all things whatsoever ye would that men should do to you, do ye even so to them; for this is the law and the prophets." (Verse 12.)

The critics are greatly divided in opinion, as to the manner in which this verse is connected with what goes before. The adverb "therefore" points backward and plainly implies dependence. In this all expositors agree. But they differ in their modes of establishing the connection, and we confess that we are not satisfied with any of these methods. We suggest with unfeigned diffidence, a different explanation from any given by the orthodox commentators. The first five verses contain a rule in regard to reproving; the sixth verse shows the impropriety of indiscriminate rebukes; the next five verses are parenthetical, and might be omitted without breaking the chain of thought. They are simply explanatory of the manner in which grace may be obtained for the exercise of the high spiritual religion enjoined by the Son of God. The 12th verse is, then, we think, linked with the first five, "Judge not, that ye be not judged, &c. For with what judgment ye judge, ye shall be judged; and with what measure ye mete, it shall be measured to you again. *Therefore* all things whatsoever ye would that men should do to you, do ye even so to them." The golden rule then shows the way of escape from the terrible retribution of God upon those who wrong their fellow-creatures. And it is in beautiful harmony with the five parenthetical verses. *They* give directions and encouragements for the attainment of the grace necessary for the practice of the rule. The whole twelve verses are thus linked and interlinked indissolubly with each other. There is moreover a close connection between the 12th verse and the 11th. We have an argument for prayer in the 11th verse, drawn from the parental relation. As parents put themselves in the places of their children, in order to enter into their sufferings and necessities; so "God was manifest in the flesh," in order to understand our trials, temptations and infirmities. "For we have not an High Priest which cannot be touched with the feeling of our infirmities; but was in all points tempted as we are, yet without sin. Let us *therefore* come boldly unto the throne of grace, that we may obtain mercy, and find grace to help in time of need." Heb. iv. 15, 16. Here Paul derives his argument for prayer, (in the same manner that his Master had done,) from the fact that God had put himself in our room, so that he might be "touched with the feeling of our infirmities." This is a favourite argument with Paul, the man of prayer. He doubtless often strengthened his own faith with it and is therefore fond of repeating it. "Wherefore in all things it behoved him to be made like unto his brethren, that he might be a merciful and faithful High Priest in things pertaining to God, to make reconciliation for the sins of the people. For in that he himself hath suffered, being tempted, he is able to succour them that are tempted." Heb. ii. 17, 18. Here Paul attributes the mercy and compassion of the Saviour towards us, to the fact that he bore our nature and endured suffering and temptation in it. The 12th verse under consideration enjoins us to do just as Christ has done; to put ourselves in the places of others; to enter fully into their trials and difficulties, their wants and sufferings, and thus be able to adapt our conduct to their condition.

We will briefly recapitulate our views in regard to the connection between the first twelve verses. We understand the golden rule of our Saviour to stand in opposition to the rule of the world, as shown in the first five verses. And it finds its sanction in the conduct of God himself, as exhibited in the 11th verse.

A few words, in explanation of the golden rule, may not be out of place. It is, of course, not to be construed literally; if the previous views be correct. The judge is not bound to acquit the guilty criminal, because if he himself were at the bar instead of on the bench, he would wish to be acquitted. This would be subversive of justice and destructive of the highest interests of society. Our Saviour has himself placed the proper limitation on the exercise of the golden rule, in declaring it to be the substance of "the law and the prophets." He virtually declares any conduct inconsistent with "the law and the prophets," to be also inconsistent with the rule. Thus the rich are not bound to give all their wealth to the poor, though, if their situations were exchanged, they might desire this wealth. This would destroy the right of property, which is recognized by "the law and the prophets." And so hundreds of similar cases might be given, showing the limitations on the exercise of the rule of "doing as you would be done by." We understand then, this precept of our Saviour to amount simply to this: We are, in our dealings with others, to imagine ourselves in their situation, and the conduct that would be agreeable to us in this altered condition, and at the same time consistent with reason, justice, "the law and the prophets," we must honestly and conscientiously practise towards them. The golden rule is a part of the law of God, engraven so deeply on the human heart, that sin and Satan have not been able entirely to efface it. For it has been found in some form among almost all the nations of the earth. Alexander Severus, a Roman Emperor, who had received it from the Christians, was so much pleased with the golden rule as to write it on the walls of his chamber. Surely, it ought to be as cordially approved, even by nominal Christians, as by a heathen. And it is plain that if men faithfully obeyed this noble precept, there would be no fraud, no false measures, no slander, no backbiting, no tyranny, no oppression, no wrangling, no law-suits, no wars and no bloodshed. But the golden rule will not be universally complied with, until "the earth shall be full of the knowledge of the Lord, as the waters cover the sea."

THE STRAIT GATE.

"Enter ye in at the strait gate; for wide is the gate, and broad is the way, that leadeth to destruction, and many there be which go in thereat; because strait is the gate, and narrow is the way, which leadeth unto life, and few there be that find it." (Verses 13, 14.)

Neander regards these two verses as cautionary, and intended to guard the disciples from the delusion of hoping to get to heaven in any other way than through the strait gate and narrow road of self-denial and self-sacrifice. He says, "Christ had pointed out the moral requisites for entrance into his kingdom, and the moral qualities which must mark its members. He now warns them (vs. 13, 14) against the delusion of expecting its blessings in any easier way than that he had pointed out, and also against the delusion of hoping to avoid struggle and self-denial." (*Life of Christ.*) Dr. Brown regards the verses as containing a detached exhortation, and not connected directly with the preceding paragraph. He says, "To enter in at the strait gate, is to embrace those views of truth, and duty, and happiness, which our Lord unfolds, and of which we have an admirable specimen in this discourse; and to walk in the narrow way, is habitually to regulate our temper and conduct by those views." (*Brown's Exposition.*) Adam Clarke sees a direct connection between the 13th and 14th verses and the 12th verse. His language is, "Enter in (to the kingdom of heaven) through *this* strait gate, i. e., of doing to every one as you would that he should do unto you; for this alone seems to be the strait gate our Lord alludes to."

A similar view is entertained by Olshausen. He says, "From what has been said, follows in a natural and unforced connection, the difficulty of walking in the path of self-denying love, which is represented under the figure of a narrow way, leading through a strait gate into the fortress of everlasting life." (*Olshausen on the Gospels.*) Scott and Henry seem to see no dependence of the verses under consideration upon any thing that goes before them. And we think it is common, both in written and oral comments upon them, to regard them as unconnected with any other part of the discourse. But amidst the various interpretations that have been given, there has been substantial agreement. The great truths of the text are too plain to be misunderstood. All expositors agree that the strait gate (or contracted gate, as the word means,) opens into the narrow way—the Christian's pathway to the skies; and that in all ages of the world there have been but few to tread this confined road.

"Broad is the road that leads to death,
And thousands walk together there;
But wisdom shows a narrower path,
With here and there a traveller."

The point of difference, between commentators, is in regard to the dependence of the 13th and 14th verses upon the context. The view of Brown of Haddington, seems to us the true one. "Christ and the work of regeneration, and faith by union with him, are a *strait gate*, by which we must strive to enter in; by this alone we enter into a new covenant state of grace and glory; nor can we enter it with one reigning lust." Luke xiii. 23; Isa. liv. 12. Christ is also "the way, the truth and the life;" and it is only by being conformed to him, united to him, and identified with him, that any man can walk in the narrow way that leadeth unto life. This road is strait, not in itself, but because of sin. The snares of the adversary of souls, the corruptions of our nature, and the allurements of the world, hedge it about, press down upon it, and thus make it narrow and contracted. To sinless beings it would be an exceeding broad and pleasant road. And this explains the apparent discrepancies in the teachings of the Bible, in regard to the holy walk. "My yoke is easy and my burden is light," says the Son of God. But the same holy Being again says: "Strait is the gate and narrow is the way that leadeth unto life." On the other hand, we hear, "Happy is the man that findeth wisdom, and the man that getteth understanding; *her ways are ways of pleasantness, and all her paths are peace.*" But once more—"He that loveth father or mother more than me, is not worthy of me; and he that loveth son or daughter more than me, is not worthy of me; *and he that taketh not his cross and followeth after me, is not worthy of me.*" And we are told that on one occasion the requirements of the gospel dispensation were so strict, that the Apostles cried out, "Lord, increase our faith;" and that on another, many of his disciples said, "This is a hard saying; who can hear it?" The whole difficulty, we see, lies in the want of faith, and in the indwelling power of sin. These make the yoke galling and the burden heavy; these make the "ways of pleasantness and the paths of peace," ways of straitness and sorrow, and paths of conflict and strife. "Ye are not straitened in me, but straitened in your own bowels," said

Paul to the Corinthians. That is, the want of sympathy between us is not from lack of affection in me towards you, but it is owing to your indifference to me. And thus, we are not straitened in Christ, but in our sinful and depraved natures. "Behold, the Lord's hand is not shortened, that it cannot save; neither his ear heavy, that it cannot hear; but your iniquities have separated between you and your God, and your sins have hid his face from you, that he will not hear." Isa. lix. 1, 2. And just as our iniquities seem to shorten the arm of God, so that it cannot save, do they seem to choke up the pathway to the skies, and make it narrow and difficult to be travelled. And these too require it to be straight as well as narrow. So great is the proneness of our fallen nature, even in its renewed state, to wander out off this straight road, that the slightest deviation to the right or to the left will lead far off from the celestial city. Christian and Hopeful, in the Pilgrim's Progress, fell into the power of Giant Despair, and were shut up in Doubting Castle, when they thought to stray but a little way from the straight and narrow path. "Now the way from the river was rough, and their feet were tender by reason of their travels; so the souls of the pilgrims were much discouraged because of the way. Wherefore, still as they went on, they wished for a better way. Now, a little before them there was, on the left hand of the road, a meadow, and a stile to go over into it; and that meadow is called *By-path Meadow.* 'Then,' said Christian, 'if this meadow *lieth along by our wayside*, let us go over into it.' But this way that seemed to lie almost parallel with the straight road, led them farther and farther off, amidst pitfalls and perilous floods, until they found themselves in a very dark dungeon, nasty and stinking to the spirits of these men." (*John Bunyan.*) Hence the Scriptures warn us against making the slightest deflection from the straight way that leads to life. "Let thine eyes look right on, and let thine eyelids look straight before thee. Ponder the path of thy feet, and let all thy ways be established. *Turn not to the right hand nor to the left;* remove thy foot from evil." Prov. iv. 25–27. And thus we see that keeping in the pathway is necessary to keeping from evil; and this necessity is founded upon the depravity of our natures; our sins make the path of life both narrow and straight. It may be that sinless creatures, from other worlds, may be permitted, in their journey to their Father's mansion, to wander in pleasant meadows, in fragrant groves, by purling brooks, and by sweet fountains. But poor fallen man is not allowed to pluck any flowers and fruits, except those that grow by the wayside. Blessed be God, there are enough of these to delight the eye, to cheer the heart and strengthen the frame of the lone pilgrim in his dusty travel.

Having adopted Brown's explanation of the terms employed in the 13th and 14th verses, we will next attempt to show their connection with the previous subject. The 12th verse briefly sums up the whole of the Christian's duty to his fellow-creatures. It consists in doing to them as he would that they should do to him. This duty has been perfectly performed by but one solitary being of our whole apostate race. The "Man of Sorrows" alone has complied with it. And just in proportion to our conformity to him, will be our obedience to the golden rule. If our union with him were perfect, so would be our compliance with the direction to "do as we would be done by." The failure to come up to this lofty standard of duty arises entirely from our not being "dead unto sin, and alive unto God through Christ Jesus our Lord." The 12th verse requires us to love our neighbours as ourselves; the 13th verse teaches us that this can only be done by having "the love of God shed abroad in our hearts by the Holy Ghost." Love to God is the only true source of love to man; and so the Apostle felt when he said, "Beloved, if God so loved us, we ought also to love one another." Paul's affection for the Corinthians was so lively, and his zeal for their spiritual well-being so vehement, that his enemies charged him with being "beside himself." But he explained his ardent interest in them by saying, "The love of Christ constraineth us." An eloquent writer has enlarged the same thought: "Here, then, is love—that deep sense of God's love to us, which shows us the necessity, the reasonableness of being kind to others; the feeling of a heart which, labouring under a sense of its obligations to God and finding itself too poor to extend its goodness to him, looks around and gives utterance to its exuberant gratitude in acts of kindness to man."

(*J. A. James.*) So intimate is the relation between the love of God and the love of man, that the Apostle expresses them both by the single word, "charity." The existence of the one species of love is a sure proof of the existence of the other. Hence, when the young man came running and kneeled down at the feet of Jesus, saying, "Good Master, what shall I do that I may inherit eternal life?" our Saviour questioned him only in regard to his obedience to the second table of the law; for if he truly loved his neighbour as himself, he might be assured that he loved God with all his heart. But though the young man thought that he had kept all the commandments of the second table "from his youth up," he "went away grieved," when he found how "exceeding broad" they were. He lacked the love of God, the only true foundation of love for man. The Apostle John, like our Saviour, makes obedience to the second table a test of obedience to the first. "We know that we have passed from death to life, because we love the brethren. He that loveth not his brother, abideth in death." "If a man say, I love God, and hateth his brother, he is a liar; for he who loveth not his brother whom he hath seen, how can he love God, whom he hath not seen? And this commandment have we from him, That he who loveth God, love his brother also." This correlation of the love of God and the love of man, establishes the connection between the 13th verse and the preceding.

A few practical thoughts are suggested by the two

gates and the two ways. Every one of our race has passed through one of these gates and is at this very instant in the road to heaven or in the road to hell. There is no third gate, there is no third path. The Son of God has proclaimed, "he that is not with me is against me." There can be no neutrality in the war raging between the powers of light and the powers of darkness. Every human being is arrayed either on the side of truth and holiness, or on the side of falsehood and wickedness. Every human being is fighting for his Maker, Redeemer, Preserver and Benefactor, or for the enemy of God, the enemy of his race and the enemy of his own soul. Every one who is united to Christ, is in the way to life, for Christ is "the way, the truth and the life." Every one who is not so united, is, at this present moment, in the broad road that leadeth to death. "He that believeth on Him (the Son) is not condemned; but he that believeth not, *is condemned already*, because he hath not believed in the name of the only begotten Son of God." Surely this consideration is solemn enough to make the most careless sinner stop in his downward course to the chambers of eternal death. "O that men were wise, that they understood this," that they would but consider that they are either in the road to God, to heaven and eternal life, or in the broad way to Satan, to hell and eternal death.

This way is broad. There is room enough in it for the hypocrite's path with all its crooks and windings. There is room enough in it for the sanctimonious self-deceiver and the bold blasphemer; for the decent moralist and the filthy rake; for the miser and the spendthrift; for the shrivelled prostitute and the modest maiden, who loves the world more than her Saviour; for the hardened old reprobate with his hands steeped in blood, and the lovely youth "not far from the kingdom of God," but still not in the way of life. All these, of various characters and dispositions, can travel together this exceeding wide road, without jostling one another. The rigid formalist, who stickles for creeds and modes of worship, but denies the power of godliness, may pursue his route to endless despair, without fearing encounter from the poor "fool," who "says in his heart, There is no God." The heretic, and the orthodox in profession, but not in life, have space enough for their different roads to everlasting torment. The brutal pagan, and the refined Christian, with enlightened understanding and unrenewed heart, has each his appropriate walk, leading with equal certainty to "where the worm dieth not and the fire is not quenched."

There is a multitude in the broad way to destruction; "many there be which go in thereat." "Hell has enlarged herself and opened her mouth without measure; and their glory, and *their multitude* and their pomp, and he that rejoiceth, shall descend into it." The multitude in the way of death draw vast crowds with them. There is a demoralizing influence in all large collections of men. This is exerted in a fourfold manner. First: They "encourage" one another, "in an evil matter." They mutually tempt and stimulate one another to sin. They commit daring, heaven-defying sins in the presence of their wicked associates, which they would be afraid to commit when alone. Herod feared John the Baptist, "knowing that he was a just man," but when surrounded by his "lords, high-captains and chief estates of Galilee," he did not hesitate to order the execution of the great forerunner of Christ. Second: The desire of the approbation of guilty companions is a strong incentive with the wicked to the commission of sin. Men often profess to be more hardened, more shameless and more depraved than they really are, for the sake of the notoriety that it gives them with their confederates in vice. "The workers of iniquity boast themselves." There is far more hypocrisy outside of the church than in it. There are more who pretend to be viler than they are, than who profess to be holier than they are. The former class of hypocrites is the more despicable of the two. The sanctimonious deceiver has, at least, some regard for decency; the other glories in his shame. Third: Sympathy with the masses is a powerful element of evil. "As in water, face answereth to face; so the heart of man to man." We are all prone to imitate the conduct of others and to be affected by feelings similar to theirs. And since the majority in every community are not on the Lord's side, the influence exerted through sympathy must, on the whole, be against the Redeemer's kingdom. Hence the wise man, in view of this, says, "enter not into the path of the wicked, and go not in the way of evil men." And He, who knows the heart of man altogether, has given this positive command, "thou shalt not follow a multitude to do evil." To the contaminating power of sympathy with evil-doers, is to be ascribed the awful depravity of large cities. Hence too, the low standard of morals among soldiers and sailors. Hence also, the greater amount of wickedness in State Universities and in Colleges overflowing with numbers, than in those less known and less celebrated. This accounts too, as we think, for the numerous rebellions and backslidings of the children of Israel in their journey to the promised land. "The mixed *multitude* fell a lusting." This explains what otherwise seems inexplicable. We wonder that a people could forget God, who had seen so many tokens of his power, and who had the pillar of cloud hovering over them by day and the pillar of fire lighting up their camp by night. But when we reflect that more than 600,000 warriors, with their families, marched under the banners of Moses and Aaron, we can readily conceive that the discontented, the murmuring and the rebellious, might touch a chord whose pulsations would be felt throughout that vast host.

The fourth evil influence exerted by the multitude, which we will notice, is that inspired by confidence in numbers. Let poor worms of the dust, who sprung up yesterday and will be crushed down to-morrow, be collected together in great crowds, and they will lift up their puny heads and feel too strong for the Omnipotent Jehovah. The angel of the Lord smote in one night, one hundred and eighty-five thousand of the host of Sennacherib, because by his messengers he had reproached the Lord, saying, "with the multitude of my chariots I am come up to the heights of the mountains, to the sides of Lebanon, and will cut down the tall cedars thereof, and the tall fir-trees thereof, &c." The horrible blasphemies, during the French Revolution, were uttered chiefly in Paris and the large cities of France. Infidelity has never flourished in rural districts; it needs to have its courage stimulated by clubs, associations and gatherings of men. Hence the good and great of our race, those who have left a healthful impress upon society, have generally been born in the country, away from the noxious influence of the multitude.

Well may the road to death be broad, since the vast crowds now in it of every sect, kindred, tongue and people, are constantly swelling their numbers, and crying out for more room. According to this view, the road is wide to accommodate the multitudes which throng it, and not to make it pleasant and agreeable. The common interpretation is, that the broad way signifies the ease with which sinners travel to destruction. This exposition conflicts with the word of God. Eternal truth has proclaimed, "the *way* of transgressors is hard." It may be wide, (and so is the path across the wastes of Sahara,) but it will be hard and painful. "Fools, because of their transgression, are afflicted." "The wicked are like the troubled sea when it cannot rest, whose waters cast up mire and dirt. There is no peace, saith my God, to the wicked." It is surely a mistake to suppose that the sinner has a happy journey to hell. He has to war against the Spirit of God, against the monitions of conscience, against the warnings of the Bible, against the remonstrances of friends, and against the pleadings of the Gospel ministry. Sinful indulgences, too, will bring loss of health, loss of property, loss of reputation, and loss of friends; so that the broad way to death will be anything but delightful. Above all, the fierce anger of God will be upon him, and "he will be cursed in the city and cursed in the field. The Lord shall send upon him cursing, vexation and rebuke, in all that he sets his hand unto for to do, until he be destroyed, and until he perish quickly; because of the wickedness of his goings." The poor sinner has lamentation and woe by the way, weeping and wailing, and gnashing of teeth at his journey's end. He is then appropriately called a "fool," by "the only wise God;" since he deliberately selects a route of travail and trouble, which leads to unending and immeasurable woe.

We think that the 14th verse contains the precious doctrine of the final perseverance of God's people. It exhorts to enter the narrow way, because there are few that find it. The language implies that the difficulty in getting to heaven consists in finding the right road. Many seek, and find not, because they seek amiss; or they seek when it is too late, as is shown in the parallel passage in Luke. Now since the whole force and life-blood of the exhortation consists in the fact, that multitudes miss the way, and not in that they stray out of it, when once in, the most natural construction that can be put upon the words of our Saviour is, that there is perfect security to the man who is united to him. They are then born of the Spirit, and "that which is born of the Spirit, is spirit." The believer has become a partaker in the nature of Christ, and God will not permit the world, the flesh, and the devil, to destroy a part of his own Son. The regenerate are gifts from the Father to the Son; and He, who has received these gifts, has said, "My Father, which gave them me, is greater than all; and no man is able to pluck them out of my Father's hand." Mere earthly monarchs will not permit their gifts to be despised; shall the Sovereign of the universe be less jealous of his? The puny kings of the world will not suffer their children to be robbed; shall the King of kings and Lord of lords be indifferent to the interests of his well-beloved Son? Some of the most desolating wars in the annals of history, have been waged to secure to the heir-apparent, his rightful possessions. The common sentiment of mankind pronounces these wars just and righteous. Ought not that sentiment also to pronounce it just, in the omnipotent God, not to allow

Christ, "whom he hath appointed heir of all things," to be deprived of the precious, immortal souls which have been given him?

FALSE GUIDES.

"Beware of false prophets, which come to you in sheep's clothing, but inwardly they are ravening wolves." (Verse 15.)

The primary signification of the word "prophet," is "one, who foretells future events." It, however, no doubt, means in this place, a religious teacher, as it does in several other places in the New Testament. Thus John says, "many false prophets are gone out into the world." And Paul speaks of those who "are built upon the foundation of the apostles and prophets, Jesus Christ being the chief corner-stone." And in writing to the Ephesians, he alludes to the "mystery of Christ" being "now revealed unto his holy apostles and prophets by the Spirit." When this was written, the spirit of prophecy, in the sense of foretelling, had almost ceased. One of the functions of the prophets was to teach; and when the gift of foretelling was taken away, the office of teaching alone remained. Peter alludes to this—"But there were false prophets among the people," (of old time,) "even as there shall be false teachers among you." Here the teacher of the new dispensation is compared with the prophet of the old. It is probable that our Saviour used the word *prophet* in the 15th verse, in its most comprehensive sense, to embrace both the false teacher in regard to future events, and the false teacher of religious truth. The "sheep's clothing," in this verse, refers to the outward profession of the teacher in holy things, which gives promise of lamb-like meekness, innocence and purity.

The dependence of the 15th verse upon the preceding, must be apparent to the most careless reader. The true reason why many do not find the narrow way, is that false guides lead them away from it into other paths. Men love to be led; and they will take any leader rather than seek the road to heaven themselves. We will not search for ourselves, and such is the perversity of our natures, that we will take any guide, in preference to the Spirit of truth, and the Book of all truth. This perverse nature we have inherited from our great progenitors, who put themselves under the guidance of Satan, and followed him rather than God. Partly from a like perversity, and partly from indolence and consequent unwillingness to search for ourselves "the Scriptures, which are able to make" us "wise unto salvation, through faith which is in Christ Jesus," we take as our guides the dicta of men, the traditions of the elders, &c. And these two powerful causes, viz. the perversity of depraved nature and natural indolence, operate to make one half of Christendom content to submit their judgments and their consciences to the control of a poor old man at Rome. The blind obedience inculcated by Catholicism to creeds, confessions of faith, formularies of the church, decisions of councils, and bulls of the

Pope, is in direct conflict with the teachings of the Son of God, and his chosen apostles. He did not even require belief in himself, except on evidence of the divine character of his mission. Therefore, he constantly referred to his miracles as proofs that he was from God. Therefore, he constantly enjoined the study of the Scriptures, that men might believe him to be the Messiah. "Search the Scriptures, for in them ye think ye have eternal life: and they are they which testify of me." We are told that "the common people heard him gladly," when he had confounded the Scribes and Pharisees by a quotation from the Psalms of David. At Nazareth, he demonstrated his Messiahship, by reading the prophecy of Esaias concerning himself. And when he ended by saying, "this day is this Scripture fulfilled in your ears; all bare him witness, and wondered at the gracious words which proceeded out of his mouth." "The chief priests and the Scribes sought to lay hands on him," when he predicted his rejection by the Jewish nation, in fulfilment of the prophecy, that "the stone which the builders rejected," was to "become the head of the corner." He often spoke of his death to the disciples, as being necessary that the Scriptures might be fulfilled. And after his resurrection, when he appeared to the two disciples, on the way to Emmaus, "beginning at Moses and all the prophets, he expounded unto them in all the Scriptures the things concerning himself." Now, since our Saviour thus constantly submitted his claims as a divine Teacher, and the truth of his doctrine, to the infallible word of God, the Protestant world have surely high authority for maintaining the right of private judgment in matters of religious belief. If Christ did not condemn, but on the contrary, approved the application of the test of the Scriptures to his life and preaching, we are disposed to think that there can be no great sin in applying the same test to the utterances of his Holiness, the Pope. Our Saviour, so far from requiring implicit trust in the teachings of religious teachers, has warned us to "beware," lest there be "false prophets," and that we be able to discern the true from the false. He has given us this

TEST OF RELIGIOUS TEACHERS.

"Ye shall know them by their fruits. Do men gather grapes of thorns, or figs of thistles? Even so every good tree bringeth forth good fruit; but a corrupt tree bringeth forth evil fruit. A good tree cannot bring forth evil fruit, neither can a corrupt tree bring forth good fruit." (Verses 16–18.)

We understand by "fruit," primarily the doctrine of the teacher. The fruit of the tree is that which it yields for the use of man. When we speak of the fruit of the labour of any one, we mean the result of his efforts in the department to which he belongs. Thus the fruit of the physician is the diseases he has cured, or the deaths he has caused. The fruit of the lawyer consists in the wrongs he has redressed, or the litigation he has fomented. The fruit of the mechanic consists in the good or bad work done in his trade. And so the fruit of the teacher is the sound or unsound instruction that he has imparted. The tree, we understand, then, to be the teacher, and the fruit to be his doctrine. The man is to be judged by his doctrine, and not the doctrine by the man. The former is the scheme of our Saviour and his Apostles, the latter of Papacy. With the Catholic, the bulls of Pio Nino must be infallible, *because* he is Pope. The fruit must be good, since they believe the tree to be good. Hence the faith of the Papist destroys all investigation, destroys all intellectual effort, and must tend to degrade him to the level of the unthinking brute. The natural result of this false scheme has been to sink Catholic countries in the scale of humanity. Paralyze the mind in regard to the examination of the most momentous questions that can interest man, and you must unfit the faculties for any rational investigation whatever. Hence the low grade of Spain, Portugal, Italy, Austria, Mexico and South America, among the thinking nations of the earth. On the other hand, the free spirit of inquiry in religious matters has made Scotland the mother of the profoundest thinkers of the earth. The open Bible, the right to read it, the right to interpret it, the right to measure all human teaching by it, the right to compare truth with truth, the right to harmonize the whole, by enlightened private judgment, and not by the arbitrary decrees of Popes and councils—these glorious privileges have placed Scotland in the fore-front of the intellectual world. These high and holy privileges have been guarantied to her too, not by princes and nobles of the earth, but by the Scriptures of truth. "My beloved," says John, "believe not every spirit, but try the spirits, whether they be of God." Language cannot be constructed plainer, to show that the trial of religious instructors is to be made by believers themselves, and for themselves. But a greater than John had taught that men must take heed for themselves, and judge false teachers by themselves. "For false Christs and false prophets shall arise," said our Saviour, "and shall show signs and wonders, to seduce, if it were possible, even the elect. But take ye heed: behold, I have foretold you all things." Mark xiii. 22, 23. The personality of the address cannot be mistaken; believers are not to trust to the guardianship of others, but are to be on their own guard, and whilst thus watching, are to escape the snares of seducers, by observing the precautions their Master has given them. Here, then, we will leave the matter. The example of our Saviour, in submitting his own claims to the Scripture ordeal, and his warning to his disciples, to beware of false prophets, and to take heed of seducers, these are sufficient to prove that we have a right to think for ourselves, and to examine all religious teaching in the light of God's word. The caution, too, against "blind guides" and "false prophets," is in itself a caution against their wrong guidance and wrong instruction; just as a warning against an unskilful surgeon would be a warning against his mal-practice. So Peter denounces "false teachers," because they "privily shall bring in *damnable heresies*, even denying the Lord that bought them." So Paul tells Timothy, that "the Spirit speaketh expressly, that in the latter times some shall depart from the faith, giving heed to seducing spirits and *doctrines of devils*." The danger then lies in the doctrine; it is this that constitutes the evil, it is this that is to be avoided, it is this that is to show the corruptness of the tree. A feeble objection may be raised to this view, on the ground that bad men may preach the truth. If so, their teaching ought to be laid up in the heart, and practised in the life of the hearer. On the other hand, may not a proclaimer of the most atrocious heresies be outwardly circumspect and blameless in all his walk and conversation? It has often been said, that the Socinianism of one of our largest and most enlightened cities, was due to the respect felt for the pure character, as well as great talents, of a popular preacher of that doctrine. And it is plain, that the more blameless the life of the heresiarch, the more dangerous will be the heresy. We think, then, that "the fruit" must primarily refer to the instruction and not to the conduct and behaviour of the "false prophet." If Satan can transform himself into an angel of light, much more may a less sinful mortal bear the outward semblance of rectitude and propriety. Still, in a subordinate sense, the fruit may, and most probably does, refer to the works of the teacher. If he be a man of known bad character, it is strong *prima facie* evidence that his doctrine is wrong, and we should be specially on our guard in receiving it. We should weigh it well, and examine it well, by the only true criterion of orthodoxy, God's infallible word.

The figure, employed by our Saviour, of the good and the bad tree, is very suggestive; but like other figures, it may be made to convey a meaning which cannot be deduced legitimately from it. Some have thought that the doctrine of human perfectibility was taught in the sentence, "a good tree *cannot* bring forth evil fruit." Adam Clarke says, "to teach as some have done, that a state of salvation can consist with the greatest crimes, (such as murder and adultery in David,) or that the righteous necessarily sin in all their best works, is really to make the good tree bring forth bad fruit, and to give the lie to the Author of eternal truth." (*Clarke on the 18th verse.*) Now, it is well known, as before stated, that men do not judge of a tree by a single bearing, but by its yield during a course of years. Still less, do they judge the tree by a few specimens, whether good or bad, in a single bearing. Some kinds of trees, (as the peach,) produce, when far gone in decay, a handful of their most delicious fruit. Surely these half-dead and half-barren trees would not be pronounced good. If then a tree is not called good, because it yields a little choice fruit in a single year, neither should it be called bad, though it should fail altogether, one summer, to yield its delicious products. In fact, it ought not to be called bad, though it should even bear some bad fruit every season. The noblest trees in the orchard cast a large amount of untimely fruit. No one ever yet saw a fruit-tree that did not have along with its rich treasures a goodly proportion of crude, dwarfish, worm-eaten fruit. And so, no one ever knew a Christian, who did not bring forth some fruit "not meet for the Master's use." Let the perfectionists point to a single sinless man, who has lived, moved, and had being in this sinful world. They will then exhibit such an one, as God, "whose eyes are in every place," has never been able to behold. Psalm xiv. From the manner, too, in which He speaks of Noah, Daniel, and Job, in the 14th chapter of Ezekiel, it is fair to infer that he regarded them as the holiest of all his creatures. And yet, the intemperance of the first, and the penitent confessions from the lips of the last two, forbid us to suppose that even these mighty men of the Lord were free from the pollution of sin. Dr. Clarke might have learned a different lesson from the very symbol which has misled him. A killing frost frequently nips the blossoms, the buds and the fruit of the finest trees in the orchard; so the blighting influence of "the Prince of the power of the air," but too often renders unproductive, for a time, the noblest vines in the vineyard of the Lord. Moreover, an instructive truth is taught us by the mode in which the good tree is blighted for a season. The withering frost comes arrayed in white, the emblem of innocence, and it robes the plant it means to injure, in a lovely and attractive garb. And so the sin, that destroys the Christian's fruit, comes generally in some seducing guise. Thus James and John, when indulging the most malignant feelings towards a village of the Samaritans, thought that they were but jealous for the honour of their Master. Thus, honest and conscientious persecutors, in every age of the world, have covered up their rancour and virulence, under cover of zeal for the Lord. Thus, Saul thought that he was doing God service, when giving the reins to his venomous hate. Thus, too, it is with the well-meaning fanatics of the present day, who disguise their bitter enmity to their brethren, under the mask of false philanthropy. How often has the pretext of innocent amusements seduced to the theatre, to the gaming-table, and to the haunts of vice! How often has the young disciple put forth fair leaves and buds of promise, but alas, has had his fruit blasted by some white-robed temptation! How often has some alluring vice assumed the semblance of virtue, to delude the old and well-established Christian!

THE VINE AND THE FIG-TREE.

These objects were familiar to all his hearers, and, we presume, that this was the chief reason why our Saviour employed them, to illustrate his warning against false prophets. And thus it is in all his wonderful teaching; all his figures, types and emblems are drawn from every-day life, and are, therefore, within the comprehension of the humblest of mankind. The vine and the fig-tree abounded in Palestine, and were familiar to all his audience. They were accustomed, moreover, to see them associated together in the writings of Moses and the prophets. We find them thus associated in the description of the promised land—"a land of wheat and barley, and vines and fig-trees, and pomegranates; a land of oil-olive and honey." Deut. viii. 8. Dwelling securely under the vine and fig-tree was typical of peace, prosperity and plentifulness. Thus, it is said, that during the reign of Solomon, "Judah and Israel dwelt safely, every man under his vine and under his fig-tree." 1 Kings iv. 24. And the crowning blessing of the restoration shall be, that "they shall sit every man under his vine and under his fig-tree; and none shall make them afraid." Micah iv. 4. And in the curse denounced by Jeremiah for their disobedience, it was predicted that their enemies should "eat up their vines and their fig-trees." It was the pathetic lament of Joel, "that a nation, strong and without number, hath laid my vine waste, and barked my fig-tree." We find the vine and the fig-tree mentioned together in the sublime hymn-prayer of Habakkuk, and in many other places in the Old Testament Scriptures. So that our Saviour alludes to them, not merely because his disciples were familiar with the objects themselves, but because they were also familiar with the typical character which they bore in the writings of Moses and the prophets. This familiarity with symbolic language, would make the audience readily comprehend any new use made of these plants, in conveying moral instruction. But we can readily conceive other reasons for using the vine and the fig-tree, rather than any others of the growth of the forest, to prefigure all the instruction which Christ wished to convey. First, since there is a thorn that has a berry not unlike the grape, and since there is a thistle that has a pod not unlike the fig, the point of the warning against false teachers, is not to trust in outward appearance. Heresy may resemble orthodoxy; bad doctrine is often very like to good; corrupt, worm-eaten fruit can scarcely be distinguished on the outside, from the sound and healthful. Moses speaking of the wicked says, "their vine is the vine of Sodom." It is thought that in his day, the fruit which grew on the coasts of the Dead Sea, though outwardly beautiful, were all rotten within, and "turned to ashes on the lips." The poet Moore has embalmed this idea, in some exquisite lines. The fact, that our Saviour speaks of products that so closely resemble the bearing of the vine and the fig-tree, is sufficient to show that dangerous forms of error may present a seeming family likeness to the truths of God. The sons of the prophets mistook poisonous wild gourds for nutritious garden vegetables. Thus the most pernicious instruction may bear the similitude of inspired teaching. Mahomet threw a patch-work covering of Judaism and Christianity, over his hideous system of religion, and thus concealed its monstrous features. Since, then, the true and the false, the sound and the unsound, the beautiful and the shocking, in religious teaching, may be made to look so much alike, how important it is, to "try the spirits, whether they be of God."

Second. We are taught by the figure, dependence upon God. The vine, to which the believer is so often likened in the Scriptures, is a dependent plant. It can never rise above the ground, and must for ever creep along there, unless it lay hold with its tendrils upon something of sturdier growth. If it wrap itself around the majestic oak, with broad-spreading branches, it too will send out its creepers far and wide, and it will fall only when the giant of the forest shall fall. But if it seize upon some frail and slender support, it will share in the insignificance of its prop, and partake of its speedy ruin. If it climb upon the tall pine, its clusters will ripen high in the air, under the genial influence of the sun. But if it attach itself to some dwarfling of the grove, it will be overshadowed and its fruit will be sour and rotten, from want of light and heat. Thus it is with man; if he cling to the earth, he will be a groveller and creeper all the days of his wretched existence. But if he take Jesus as his prop and support, he will ever be rising higher and higher towards heaven and God, and his fruit will be unto eternal life.

Third. The figure teaches the avoidance of ostentation and display. The vine and the fig-tree have no gaudy flowers to attract the eye and please the fancy. The vine, when in bloom, fills the surrounding atmosphere with its fragrance. But this perfume literally steals upon the air; the modest giver can only be found after diligent search, embowered from observation in some leafy covert. And thus it should be with the child of God; the odour of his holy life should be breathed by all in his atmosphere, while he himself is in retirement from prying gaze and noisy applause.

Fourth. The figure teaches that the disciple of Christ should be fruitful. The fig-tree is his type, and it is among the most fruitful trees of the earth. The celebrated botanist and traveller, Tournefort, says, that he saw fig-trees in the islands of the Archipelago, which yielded two hundred and eighty pounds of fruit apiece annually. The fig-tree is then eminently fruitful and useful, though it has so little in its appearance of the splendid and the gorgeous. And thus should it be with the Christian; all his powers should be devoted to usefulness, and not to selfish and vainglorious display.

Fifth. The figure teaches the nature of grace—free, sovereign, electing grace. The vine and the fig-trees in the vineyard and orchard, are the planting of the husbandman, who selects the scions according to his pleasure. He selects, plants, waters, and nurtures just such plants as he thinks will suit his purpose the best. And thus it is with the Great Husbandman,

He chooses, in his sovereign pleasure, some for honour and some for dishonour, some for one service and some for another, and some are passed by or rejected altogether. And as the shoots chosen by the husbandman have no cause for boasting and self-laudation, neither have the elect of God any cause to glory in their selection. The reason of it is to be found in his gracious will, and not in their deserving of this special mark of his consideration. The honour calls for humility, gratitude, and the thankful acknowledgment, "even so, Father, for so it seemed good in thy sight." The Jews were chosen from among all the nations of the earth, not because of their merits, but because of the grace of God. And so he has selected from among the Gentiles, of his own free will, wild-olive branches, to partake of "the root and fatness of the olive-tree." Rom. xi. 17. And those plants alone which he has put in the soil, or grafted into good trees, will bear fruit unto eternal life. "Every plant," says our Saviour, "which my heavenly Father hath not planted, shall be rooted up."

Although it has but little connection with the present subject, it may not be amiss to state, that the figure of grafting, employed by St. Paul, explains perfectly what seem to some anomalies in the character of the renewed man. The world often expects the individual, who professes "to be born again," to be "a new creature," not merely in the principles and motives that actuate him, but also in temperament and disposition. But the language of Paul teaches a different lesson. The juices flow into the grafted scion through the old channel; but *the juices themselves are different*, and they convert the wild and noxious fruit into the useful and the healthful. And thus it is with the renewed child of God. He retains his old temperament, his old disposition, his old mental organization, and his old physical nature; but a living God-sent vitality permeates them all, and changes hurtful lusts into holy desires, persecuting zeal into ardent philanthropy, energy for evil into activity for good, love for error into devotion to truth, delight in sensual indulgence into joy in spiritual worship, audacity in upholding the wrong into courage in defending the right, sanguine trust in the world to hopeful confidence in God, persevering effort to accomplish wicked ends into consistent diligence to be useful. Thus John retained his loving disposition, Peter his impetuous temperament, Paul his fiery zeal, Nicodemus his prudence, and Zaccheus his low stature. The great change leaves unaltered the usual channels of thought, of feeling, and of action. The learned does not become unlearned, neither does the simple become wise in the wisdom of this world; the hopeful does not become despondent, nor is the melancholy temperament necessarily changed into the sanguine and the cheerful. Grace modifies the tone of thought, and the natural temperament, just so far as is necessary for the glory of God and no farther. The harp that gives out its music to his praise is composed of many strings. At one time it is struck by lamenting Jeremiah, and wails out the melancholy strain, "I am the man that hath seen affliction by the rod of his wrath. He hath led me, and brought me into darkness, but not into light. Surely against me is he turned; he turneth his hand against me all the day." Again, it is struck by Miriam and her rejoicing attendants, and utters in tones of triumph: "Sing ye unto the Lord, for he hath triumphed gloriously; the horse and his rider hath he thrown into the sea." And so the penitential psalm and the hymn of praise has each its appropriate string, and its appropriate tune. Who can tell whether the melody of contrition or the melody of gratitude be most grateful to the great Author of our lives? Who can tell whether the deep diapason of trust in him, or the lowly music of self-loathing and self-distrust, strikes most harmoniously on "the ears of the Lord of Sabaoth"? Who can tell whether the swelling notes of the confident and the impetuous, or the plaintive tones of the diffident and the cautious, be most agreeable to him? Who can tell whether he is most pleased with the war-cry of Mr. Great-Heart, or with the timid yet loving appeal of Mr. Feeble-Mind? Doubtless, he has given a diversity of gifts and tongues, a diversity of tastes and temperaments, a diversity of thoughts and feelings, in order that the grand universal symphony, in which the whole body of believers unite, may be more varied, more rich, more full, and more sweet.

TEST OF PROFESSED DISCIPLES.

"Every tree that bringeth not forth good fruit, is hewn down, and cast into the fire. Wherefore by their fruits ye shall know them." (Verses 19, 20.)

The word "every" in these verses, evidently refers to the whole body of communicants. We understand our Saviour to give in them a test, by which professed disciples may be judged, and that is their fruitfulness. The preceding verses try religious teachers by their good or bad fruit; these, all who have taken the oath of allegiance to Christ, by their productiveness or barrenness. The former embrace the clergy, the latter the laity. We confine the application of the 19th verse to professed believers, because in the parable of the fig-tree, as recorded by Luke, (13th chapter,) it is the unfruitful tree *planted* in the *vineyard*, and not that growing wild in the forest, which is to be cut down, because of its barrenness. And we think that religious teachers are not embraced in the threat contained in the 19th verse, because *they cannot* be unfruitful. Their doctrine must be "according to godliness," else it will be "the doctrine of devils." It must have "a savour of life unto life," else it will have "a savour of death unto death." The minister of the gospel can occupy no neutral ground. But the private member of the church may be a mere negation. He may be neither cold nor hot. He may be neither on the Lord's side, nor on the side of Satan and the world. He may stimulate no one, by his holy walk and conversation, to zeal for the service of God; neither may he urge them, by word or act, to strive for the wages of iniquity. Instead of bearing bad fruit, he may lie (so the 19th verse teaches) as a *cut down tree*, a *dead log*, in the way of life, over which, it is true, multitudes may tumble into perdition. But he is then a passive, and not an active, instrument of mischief. He may however do more harm by his immobility, than the heresiarch by his activity. The dead log, across the railroad track, may be more destructive than the upas-tree, with its poisonous breath. Men are prone to look upon the decaying trunk in the way as an innocent thing; but it is an impediment and an obstruction to all, and it may be a stumbling-block to many. And thus it is with the inert, sluggish disciple. He may fancy that he wrongs no one, when he is obstructing the narrow way that leadeth to life. We understand then the test of the private member of the church to be different from that of the preacher. The latter is to be tried by the scriptural or unscriptural character of his preaching; the former by his fruitfulness or barrenness, by his activity or by his slothfulness.

FINAL DESTINY OF THE BARREN.

"Every tree which bringeth not forth good fruit, *is* hewn down and cast into the fire." The present tense and not the future is employed. The axe is already eating into the heart and life of the barren tree. The act of cutting down is now going on. The bark is even now cut, the life-giving sap is flowing out; the cells that contain it, the channels that convey it, are breaking up. And yet there is nothing to give sign that the fatal work is in progress, the axe does not ring out on the air, there is no moving in the top of the tree, the leaves are withering so slowly that the beholder cannot distinguish the incipient decay. Who can tell how far the girdling may go on and the tree still live? Who can tell when the next blow will bring crashing to the earth all those goodly but fruitless branches, with their rich but useless foliage? Who can tell whether the axe shall be arrested before the tree fall, but not until it shall be fatally injured? Who can tell how long it may be left a leafless, sapless trunk, by the way-side, robbed of that verdure which gave promise of fruit and yielded none? Who can tell how long it may stand as a monument of God's wrath—desolate, doomed, and forsaken?

The fruitless disciple should ponder it well, that he is compared to a tree, against which the blows of the woodman are falling thick and fast. A little time more, its fate will be sealed and its death certain. And though it fall not, it is left drying up to be fitter for burning.

PRUNING AND CUTTING DOWN.

The excision of the barren tree is a different thing from the pruning of the fruitful. "Every branch that beareth fruit," says our Saviour, "he (the Father) purgeth it, that it may bring forth more fruit." The pruning is to cut off those shoots, which serve as channels to carry off the juices from the main stem. When these outlets are closed up, the sap flows back into the proper ducts, and produces fruit for the husbandman's use. The affections, that ought to flow out towards God, are frequently turned from their channels into some shoot by the side, (it may be some cherished son or daughter;) but when this shoot is removed, they return to their old courses, and move on with their wonted current and vigour. The pruning of the good tree is salutary, it makes it healthful and fruitful. But every blow struck at the barren tree is a blow struck at its life. The wounds are not given for healing, but for destruction. The cutting is not to send the juices back to their old channels, but to waste them on the ground. It is not to impart fresh vitality, vigour, and beauty, but to produce disease, death, and rottenness. This explains the difference between the trials of the righteous and of the wicked. In the former, they are pruning; in the latter, girdling. In the one, the trimming of the vine-dresser to make the vine more productive; in the other, the cutting down or deadening by the farmer of the useless trees that take strength and nutriment from his crop. In the one, they are the winnowing of the chaff from the wheat to make the wheat better; in the other, the gathering of the chaff for the fire. In the one, they are the tillage of the soil; in the other, the rooting up of the tares before the time. Here then, we have a test of Christian character. Those who are made more fruitful, more heavenly-minded, more weaned from the world, by their trials, disappointments, and bereavements, have reason to hope that they have been *chastised* by a faithful and affectionate *Parent.* But those who are hardened and made more rebellious by their troubles and afflictions, have reason to fear that they have had a foretaste of *punishment* from an inexorable *Judge.* Jacob was sanctified by his multiplied afflictions, and there was a moral grandeur in the closing years of his life, which we in vain look for in his youth and early manhood; but Pharaoh hardened his neck when often reproved, and he was "suddenly destroyed, and that without remedy." David could say, "it was good for me that I have been afflicted;" but Saul was but rendered furious and desperate, by the severe judgments of a righteous God. Father in heaven, when thou layest thy hot and heavy hand on us guilty wretches, O teach us to say with the innocent Sufferer, "not my will, but thine be done." When thou cuttest the cords that bind us to this perishing earth, O that thou wouldst bind the sundered ends to thine own eternal throne.

THE SIN OF UNFRUITFULNESS.

The language of the 19th verse is very impressive. It is not the corrupt tree, but the tree which bringeth not forth good fruit, that is to be hewn down and cast into the fire. And so in the figure employed, our Saviour does not speak of *noxious plants*, such as the upas tree, but of the *barren*—the thorn, and the thistle. And this is characteristic of all our Lord's teaching. He condemns neglect of duty more frequently than positive sin; unfruitfulness more than yielding bad fruit. The burden of his parables is the sin of barrenness. The seed by the way-side, the seed among thorns, and the seed on stony ground, all represent the word received into unfruitful hearts. The householder, who let out his vineyard to husbandmen who would not render him the fruits in their season, was but a type of the Lord in his dealings with the Jewish nation, which did not render to him the peaceable fruits of righteousness. The poor wretch, at the marriage feast, *had neglected* to put on the wedding garment. The five foolish virgins *had neglected* to put oil in their lamps. The slothful servant, who hid his one talent in the earth, was cast into outer darkness for *neglecting* to put his Lord's money to the exchangers. The unprofitable servant, who laid his one pound up in a napkin, was deprived of it, because he *neglected* to put his Lord's money into the bank. In the parable of the supper, the offence was *neglecting* to come to the feast. In the parable of the fig-tree, it was to be cut down because the Lord had come for three years seeking fruit, and *finding none.* And so, too, in the vision of judgment, as given in the 25th chapter of Matthew; the offences, charged against those on the left hand, are all of them neglects of duty. "Depart from me, ye cursed, into everlasting fire prepared for the devil and his angels: for I was an hungered, and ye gave me no meat: I was thirsty, and ye gave me no drink: I was a stranger, and ye took me not in: naked, and ye clothed me not: sick, and in prison, and ye visited me not." It is remarkable, too, that the only curse pronounced by our Saviour, whilst on earth, was that against the barren fig-tree. And thus it was ever the sin of omission which he especially rebuked. "Ye *will not come* unto me that ye might have life." "O Jerusalem, Jerusalem, which killest the prophets, and stonest them which are sent unto thee; how often would I have gathered thy children together, as a hen doth gather her brood under her wings, and *ye would not.*" "For every one that doeth evil hateth the light, neither *cometh* to the light, lest his deeds should be reproved."

The reason of this special condemnation of unfruitfulness is plain. Slothful, inconsistent Christians do far more harm to the cause of religion than blaspheming infidels. The false disciple is a stone of stumbling and a rock of offence, and retributive justice makes his punishment worse than having a mill-stone about his neck, and being cast into the depth of the sea. Matt. xviii. 6. The blasphemer is like the breaker at sea; it gives warning of danger by the roar and dashing of the waves. The inert, impassive, immovable disciple is the sunken rock that wrecks, in a moment of hope and confidence, the stately vessel, with her precious freight of immortal souls.

It may be well to remark, that the 20th verse, ("wherefore by their fruits ye shall know them,") is not the mere repetition of the 16th verse. It contains rather the summary of the tests of the religious teacher, and the private member of the church. Each is to be judged by his fruits; the former by his good or bad fruit; the latter by the presence or absence of fruit. The comparison of the faithless disciple to a tree without fruit, is similar to that before given—salt which has lost its savour. In both illustrations there is semblance without reality, shadow without substance, promise of good without fulfilment.

LIP-SERVICE.

"Not every one that saith unto me, Lord, Lord, shall enter into the kingdom of heaven; but he that doeth the will of my Father which is in heaven." (21st verse.)

The leading thought contained in this verse is the same as in the preceding verses. The man who professes to honour God with his lips, and shows forth no good deeds in his life, is like the tree that has abundance of leaves and blossoms, and yields no fruit in its season. And as the husbandman is not content with the delusive foliage, neither is God content with the deceptive profession. Both planted for the fruit. Neither will be satisfied without it. God looks at the heart, not at the lips. Good works and not good words receive his commendation. The faithful servant, not the faithful talker, is rewarded with the "well done." The honest performance, and not the flattering promise, meets his approbation.

Alas, how prone men are to be satisfied with drawing nigh unto God with their mouths, when their hearts are far from him! How prone to lull their consciences to sleep with a name to live, when dead in trespasses and sins! The Jews, when wholly given up to idolatry, could boastfully exclaim, "The temple of the Lord, the temple of the Lord, are these." And when their hearts were fully set in them to do evil, it is said of them, that "Bethel was their confidence," and that they were "haughty because of the holy mountain." And thus it is with thousands and tens of thousands at the present day. They boast in the church, and glory in their Christian profession, while practically denying, by their walk and conversation, the power of godliness and the beauty of holiness. And just in proportion to the hollowness of their hearts is the noisiness of their tongues. It is the hollow bell, and not the solid metal, which gives out most sound. Thorns crackle more under the pot than substantial hickory. Dry thistles and straw throw out more blaze than oak and ash. The shallow brook babbles incessantly, the deep river flows on in perpetual silence. Peter was the only one of the disciples who was loud in professions of unwavering allegiance to his Master; and Peter was the only one of the disciples who denied his Lord. Judas was the only one of the apostles who talked generously of giving to the poor; and Judas was the only thief in the apostolic band. We read of but one kiss being given to our blessed Redeemer; and that kiss was from the lips of a traitor. We read in the Scriptures of but one man who boasted of his zeal for the Lord, and that man was the profligate idolator Jehu.

In his last discourse on earth, our Saviour was careful to draw a broad line of distinction between doing and saying, practice and profession, heart-service and lip-service. "He that abideth in me and I in him, the same bringeth forth much fruit." "Herein is my Father glorified, that ye bear much fruit." "If ye keep my commandments, ye shall abide in my love." "Continue ye in my love." "Ye are my friends, if ye do whatsoever I command you." "Ye have not chosen me, but I have chosen you, and ordained you, that ye should go and bring forth fruit." Here the highest possible reason is given for the performance of good deeds. They are not to merit salvation, but to glorify God. He is honoured by the good fruit of his vineyard, just as the husbandman is honoured by an abundant yield from his cultivated grounds.

JESUS DECLARES HIS MESSIAHSHIP.

The 21st verse is remarkable as containing the first declaration, in this sermon, of the Messiahship of the illustrious speaker. Previously he had spoken as one having superior authority to the Jewish teachers, and he had calmly set aside their false doctrine, and interposed his own majestic, "but I say unto you." Now, however, he speaks as one to whom the veil, that shrouds the world of spirits, had been lifted; as one who knew the final destiny of every human being. We may imagine with what indignation the proud Scribes and Pharisees listened to the despised Nazarene, the carpenter's son, as he exposed the falsity of their instruction, and the corruptness of their practice. But now astonishment must have swallowed up every other emotion, when this man, who had no pretension to learning, (John vii. 15,) professed to be able to read God's book of life, and to know who would be saved and who would be lost. And how must that astonishment have increased, when he went on (22d verse) to unfold the scenes of the great day of judgment, and to describe men as appealing *to him* to be saved, because of the mighty works done in *his* name. And finally, their amazement must have passed all bounds, when the lowly Galilean spake with calm dignity of himself as the Judge of the quick and dead, (23d verse.) Who can form any adequate conception of this whole scene? There stands a supposed illiterate peasant, a native of a despised community; a few ignorant fishermen are his friends and followers, and now sit reverentially at his feet; while right before him are the proud, the powerful, the learned, and the respected Jewish rulers and teachers. He begins by addressing a few words of comfort and consolation, of warning and direction, to his humble disciples, and then launches boldly forth in condemnation of the whole religious system of the most honoured and revered sects of his nation; promulgates doctrines entirely opposed to the passions, prejudices, and principles of the whole race of mankind; and ends with giving sanction and emphasis to all that he had uttered, by announcing himself to be the "Judge of all the earth." His words must have been attended with a divine energy, they must have come home to the hearts and consciences of his hearers with demonstration of the Spirit and power; else, they would have seemed the ravings of a madman. How else can we account for the toleration of the haughty and vindictive Scribes and Pharisees, when he exposed the ostentatious, vainglorious, self-seeking character of their religion? How else can we account for the bigoted, fanatical priests refraining to arrest him, as a blasphemer, when he arrogated to himself the attributes of the great God of the universe?

SELF-DECEPTION.

"Many will say to me in that day, Lord, Lord, have we not prophesied in thy name? and in thy name have cast out devils? and in thy name done many wonderful works? And then will I profess unto them, I never knew you: depart from me, ye that work iniquity." (Verses 22, 23.)

There are six things in these verses that deserve our special consideration. First. The persons here described had made higher attainments than those mentioned in the 21st verse. These had gone much further than merely saying, "Lord, Lord," in an outward profession of religion. They had also been honoured with the gifts of prophecy, of casting out devils, and of working miracles; and yet after all were lost. Thus, "Saul was among the prophets;" Caiaphas, the cruel, malignant wretch, was endued with the spirit of prophecy; Judas, "the son of perdition," cast out devils; the Egyptian sorcerers wrought miracles. God may choose to bestow spiritual gifts upon unholy men, just as he often gives them genius and mental power. But the most wonderful endowments and the highest attainments count as nothing in his sight, if there be wanting "holiness, without which no man shall see the Lord." "Though I have the gift of prophecy, and understand all mysteries, and all knowledge; and though I have all faith, so that I could remove mountains, and have not charity, I am nothing." And so Paul feared that notwithstanding his exalted gifts and amazing success as a preacher, he himself might be lost. "But I keep under my body and bring it into subjection; lest that by any means, when I have preached to others, I myself should be a cast-away." 1 Cor. ix. 27. How different is this humble spirit of the great Apostle from that of those who profess to have arrived at perfect assurance and a sinless state!

Second. The two verses under consideration with the one immediately preceding, constitute an unanswerable argument to prove the divinity of the Saviour. In the 21st verse, he describes himself as perfectly acquainted with the secrets of the invisible world. In the 22d, he declares that he will be appealed to, as the umpire, in the great day of final accounts; and in the 23d, he teaches that it is his mandate that will banish the wicked to hell. These are attributes of God, and of God only. Hence the man of Calvary is "God manifest in the flesh."

Third. We infer that the great body of professed disciples, who are lost, are self-deceivers, and not bold, audacious hypocrites. There is something so horrible in the thought of men assuming the garb of holiness, for wicked and selfish ends, that we are not disposed to believe that there are many unworthy communicants who are conscious of their own unworthiness. They must first deceive themselves, before they can deceive the world. No actor can play a feigned part well, without first entering into its spirit. The embodiments of the fancy must become tangible realities to him, else he can throw no illusion over the minds of the spectators. He must first delude himself, else he cannot delude his audience. Just so it is with the hypocrite, the *actor*, (as the word means;) he cannot impose upon others, until he has first imposed upon himself. And how fearful it is to reflect that men may live deceived in regard to their spiritual condition, that they may die deceived, and that they may stand deceived before the very bar of God! How dreadful to think that men may die in the hope of a blessed immortality, when an eternity of torment awaits them; that they may even rise from the dead expecting to hear, "Come, ye blessed of my Father, inherit the kingdom prepared for you from the foundation of the world," when they shall only hear, "Depart from me, ye cursed, into everlasting fire, prepared for the devil and his angels!"

How important then is the duty of self-examination! How careful we should be to look well to the foundation of our hope!

"When I turn my eyes within,
All is dark, and vain, and wild;
Filled with unbelief and sin,
Can I deem myself a child?
Lord, decide the doubtful case,
Thou, who art thy people's Sun:
Shine upon thy work of grace,
If it be indeed begun.
Let me love thee more and more,
If I love at all, I pray;
If I have not loved before,
Help me to begin to-day."

Fourth. The 22d verse explains the reason of the self-deception. The persons described in it were satisfied with mere gifts and attainments, and did not trust to the righteousness of Christ. They trusted in themselves that they were righteous. Observe, that they do not say, "Lord, Lord, thou knowest how we loathed sin and hated ourselves on account of it; thou knowest how we felt our utter inability to satisfy the claims of justice; thou knowest how we despaired of doing any good thing in our own strength; thou knowest how, when we were thus convinced of our sin and misery, our minds were enlightened in the knowledge of thee, and our wills were renewed, so that we were enabled to embrace thee as our Saviour and our God." They have none of this humble spirit, none of this dependence upon a righteousness not their own. On the contrary, they are proud, boastful, self-sufficient, confident of their acceptance because of their mighty works. Therefore strong delusion was sent upon them, that they should believe a lie, in regard to the condition of their immortal souls. Their whole language shows that they knew nothing of humility, nothing of repentance, nothing of faith, and nothing of holiness.

Fifth. The 21st verse most probably refers to self-deceivers among the laity, and the 22d to self-deceivers in the ranks of the clergy. If so, the language employed intimates that there is, proportionally, a greater number of the latter than of the former. In the 21st verse, it is "not every one," (*ou pas;*) in the 22d verse, it is, "many," (*polloi.*) Nor need we be surprised at this greater proportion of self-deceivers in the gospel ministry, when we reflect that it is entered in some countries merely as "a living," and is designated by that name; that it gives a position of respectability and literary ease; that it may induce the habit of applying texts of Scripture to the wants of the congregation, and not to the minister's own individual case; that it may beget spiritual pride—trust in the sacred profession, &c. &c. However this may be, if we were called upon to name the holiest man we ever knew, we would not designate an eloquent preacher, a learned theologian, a distinguished doctor of divinity, but an illiterate African slave. We read of our Saviour rejoicing but once upon earth, and then it was because his "Father had hid these things from the wise and prudent, and had revealed them unto babes." Of like import is the language of David, "O Lord, our Lord, how excellent is thy name in all the earth! who hast set thy glory above the heavens. Out of the mouth of babes and sucklings hast thou ordained strength." Psalm viii. 1, 2. The glory of God is set above the heavens—is specially manfested by the little ones in Christ, the babes and sucklings, the lambs of the flock. The "please give me a new heart"* of the child on his dying couch, may honour him more than the eloquent prayer of Solomon before the assembly of Israel. The hymn of praise from the lowly hut may be more acceptable to him than the swelling tones of the organ in some grand old cathedral. The sweetest strains in the heavenly choir may be from the lips whose innocent prattle delighted so much on earth. Let us rejoice then in the pleasure they give our glorious Benefactor, and not selfishly mourn their loss.

Sixth. The glorious doctrine of the final persever-

* These were almost the last words of a much-loved boy.

ance of God's people is plainly recognized: "And then I will profess unto them, I *never knew* you." Those who are rejected, have never been known, approved, and recognized by God as his children. The world may have so recognized them, but he had made no such mistake. The language plainly "intimates that if he had ever known them as *the Lord knows them that are his;* had ever owned them, and loved them as his, he would have known them, and owned them, and '*loved them to the end;*' but he *never did know them;* for he always knew them to be hypocrites, and rotten at heart, as he did Judas; therefore he says, *Depart from me.*" (*Matthew Henry.*) The father can never cease to remember his earthly son; God can never cease to remember his spiritual child. The parent may have his affections alienated from his offspring; but God loves with an "*everlasting love.*" He "*changes not.*" The security of the believer rests, then, not in his own ability to persevere in holiness, but in the immutable, eternal love of God. "And I will make an *everlasting* covenant with them, that I will not turn away from them, to do them good; but I will put my fear in their hearts, that they shall not depart from me." Jer. xxxii. 40. Here we are plainly taught that the believer will never turn away from God, *because* God will never turn away from him. "Who are kept *by the power of God* through faith unto salvation." 1 Peter i. 5. The power of the Almighty God, not his own strength, is to keep the believer. The everlasting arms are beneath him; he cannot fall, until these arms become weary and fail in strength.

THE WISE MAN.

"Therefore, whosoever heareth these sayings of mine, and doeth them, I will liken him unto a wise man, which built his house upon a rock. And the rain descended, and the floods came, and the winds blew, and beat upon that house; and it fell not: for it was founded upon a rock." (Verses 24, 25.)

The figurative style, which was dropped in the three preceding verses, is now resumed. The true disciple was likened to the good tree, that gave promise of fruit by its foliage, and gave fulfilment by an abundant crop of figs and grapes. He is now likened to a wise builder, who gives promise by gathering his materials, and then fulfils by building—building well and wisely on a sure foundation.

There are several things to be specially noticed in these verses.

First. A house is a place for comfort, repose, and shelter; it stands therefore as a type of religion, to which men look for consolation and security. The rock is doubtless the rock of ages, even Christ Jesus. We learn from his own lips, that he is "the stone which the builders refused." "Other foundation," says Paul, "can no man lay than that is laid, which is Jesus Christ." 1 Cor. iii. 11. Again, the apostle writes: "And are built upon the foundation of the apostles and prophets, Jesus Christ himself being the chief corner-stone." Eph. ii. 20. But God himself speaks of his Son as the sure foundation: "Therefore thus saith the Lord God, Behold, I lay in Zion for a foundation, a stone, a tried stone, a precious corner-stone, a sure foundation: he that believeth shall not make haste." Isa. xxviii. 16. The apostle Peter calls the Saviour "a living stone, disallowed indeed of men, but chosen of God, and precious."

Since, then, the rock referred to is the rock Christ, the verses we are now considering contain an additional argument for the security of the believer. He that hath builded on *Him*, shall not be confounded. Eternal truth is pledged, that his house shall not fall, that his religion shall not fail. He is "a workman that needeth not to be ashamed." The building that he has erected *shall* stand; the tempests will roar around it, and beat upon it, in vain; the torrents will fume, and fret, and dash against it, in vain; the floods will seek to undermine it, and sap its foundation, in vain.

Second. The believer will be sorely tried; his religion will be severely tested. A storm will come, "discovering the foundation unto the neck." Hab. iii. 13. "Every man's work shall be made manifest; for the day shall declare it, because it shall be revealed by fire; and the fire shall try every man's work, of what sort it is." 1 Cor. iii. 13. The rain that descends from heaven, is most probably typical of the trials that come directly from the hand of God; such as famine, pestilence, personal sickness, loss of friends,

&c. The floods, which descended first from heaven, but have been defiled and polluted with soil and mud, most probably refer to trials permitted by God, but which are received through earthly channels; such as persecutions, slander, personal violence at the hands of the wicked, &c. &c. The tempest that beats upon the house, is surely the furious assault of "the prince of the power of the air." The believer then may expect to be tried by God, by the world, and by Satan. He has nowhere a promise of a life of ease, of freedom from trial, tribulation, and distress. His Master was "a man of sorrows, and acquainted with grief." "The servant is not better than his lord." If these things were done in the green tree, what may be expected in the dry? When John, in his vision, saw "a great multitude clothed with white robes, and palms in their hands," he was told, "these are they *which came out of great tribulation*, and have washed their robes, and made them white in the blood of the Lamb." O no! the believer has nowhere been told that his house shall not be exposed to the ravage of the flood, and the desolation of the storm. But blessed be God, he has been promised that "the gates of hell shall not prevail against it." Our great concern should not be, whether trials and afflictions await us; not whether the tempest will come; but whether we have a good building on a sure foundation, that will defy the fury of the elements, and the sweeping of the torrents.

"While I draw this fleeting breath,
When my heart-strings break in death,
When I soar to worlds unknown,
See thee on thy judgment throne,
Rock of ages, cleft for me,
Let me hide myself in thee."

"Lead me to the Rock that is higher than I." "Let not the water-flood overflow me, neither let the deep swallow me up."

"When rising floods my soul o'erflow,
When sinks my heart in waves of woe;
Jesus, thy timely aid impart,
And raise my head and cheer my heart."

Third. Not only must the foundation be of rock, but the *bond* between it and the house must be good, in order that the house may be secure. In like manner, the union must be close between Christ and the believer, so that the believer may be able to stand in the hour of trial and temptation. The two illustrations of our Saviour have then another point of resemblance. It is the union of the branch with the vine that makes it fruitful. It is the firm, indissoluble connection of the house with its foundation that makes it strong. It matters not how solid the rock may be, the building will have no stability unless it is closely bonded with that rock. It must be "fitly framed together," and fitly united to its base; there must be proportion and symmetry in all the Christian graces, and a close "sealing" to Christ, "with that Holy Spirit of promise."

THE FOOLISH MAN.

"And every one that heareth these sayings of mine, and doeth them not, shall be likened unto a foolish man, which built his house upon the sand: and the rain descended and the floods came, and the winds blew, and beat upon that house; and it fell: and great was the fall of it." (Verses 26, 27.)

These verses point backward to the 22d and 23d, and explain the nature and cause of the self-deception of the persons there described. They have a building in which they trust, but it is upon a slippery and unstable foundation. It is upon the shifting sand, not upon the immovable rock. Or, dropping the figure, they have a hope in which they trust, but this hope does not rest upon the rock Christ, and their good deeds and external morality are appropriately represented by the sand, the particles of which may be composed of the best materials; but there is no bond, no cement binding them all together, and giving them coherency, compactness, and solidity. So it is with good works which do not proceed from love for Christ. There is no life-giving principle pervading them all, and shaping them into one compact, indivisible whole. It is said of these self-deceivers, that they did mighty works in the *name*, but not in the *love* of Christ. And as the sand is liable to be drifted by every breeze, and swept away by every flood, so they are liable to be "tossed to and fro, and carried away with every wind of doctrine;"

and to be drifted off from their Christian profession by every tide of passion, prejudice, and sinful inclination.

The verses we are considering connect also both with the 17th and 18th verses. The hearer and not the doer of the word, has done a part, but the least part of his duty. He has listened to the truth. So the barren tree had done a part, but the least part of its duty. It had put forth leaves and blossoms. And as these excited the hope of abundance of fruit, so the listening to God's word gives promise of being affected and profited thereby. The tree and the man both fail to fulfil the expectations that they had created. The "end" of both "is to be burned."

Reader, may you and I "not be forgetful hearers, but doers also of the work," that we may be "blessed in our deeds." May we build our hope upon the sure rock Christ, and not upon the shifting sand of our own righteousness; that we may be fixed and stable in all our principles and actions, and not "wavering like a wave of the sea, driven with the wind and tossed." "Unto Him that is *able to keep*" *us* "*from falling*, and to present" us "faultless before the presence of his glory with exceeding joy; to the only wise God our Saviour be glory and majesty, dominion and power, both now and ever. Amen."

EFFECT UPON THE AUDIENCE.

"And it came to pass, when Jesus had ended these sayings, the people were astonished at his doctrine:

For he taught them as one having authority, and not as the Scribes." (Verses 28, 29.)

The audience were amazed, astonished, it may be awed and terrified by the dignity, boldness, and divine energy with which he spake. But we are not told that their consciences were reached, and their hearts affected by the wonderful truths which they had heard. Their understandings were enlightened in the knowledge of divine things, but we know not that the truth was received in the love of it. Probably, some of his hearers afterwards formed part of that fierce mob, which cried, "Crucify him, crucify him." But notwithstanding all this, the great doctrines proclaimed on that day, from that mountain in Galilee, have been studied, and loved, and cherished, for more than eighteen hundred years. They have been read on sea and on land, in the wilderness, and in the city, in the hovel, and in the palace. They have rebuked the proud, and given grace to the humble; they have exposed the hypocrites, and cheered the hearts of the sincere; they have brought down the lofty looks of the ostentatious, the vain, and the self-seeking, and have established the hope of the lowly in heart; they have swept away the sandy foundation of trust in self-righteousness, and have taught men to build upon the rock Christ. Yea, they have affected the sentiments, the views, the opinions, and the feelings, of the whole race of mankind. Heathen emperors have read and admired them; heathen moralists have copied them and incorporated them in their systems of religion. Poets and orators have drawn their inspiration from them; statesmen have quoted from them in their papers. Even infidels have extolled them; Rousseau has been their most eloquent panegyrist. Voltaire could find nothing in them to sneer at. Paine thought them unfit for his ribaldry. The whole earth has felt and acknowledged their influence. There is probably not a corner of it that has not received, at least some straggling rays from that bright light, which the Son of God kindled on that obscure mountain in Galilee.

Here, then, is encouragement for the gospel ministry. The poor preacher often feels with the discouraged prophet, that his preaching has been "as a very lovely song of one that has a pleasant voice, and can play well upon an instrument; for they hear the words but they do them not." Let him remember, however, that neither did his Master's sermon, so far as we know, produce any *immediate* effect. But in the end, the results have been more glorious than from the teaching of all the philosophers and all the moralists the world has ever produced. Let him remember that God has said, "for as the rain cometh down, and the snow, from heaven, and returneth not thither, but watereth the earth, and maketh it bring forth and bud, that it may give seed to the sower, and bread to the eater: so shall my word be that goeth forth out of my mouth; it shall not return unto me void, but it shall accomplish that which I please, and it shall prosper in the thing whereto I sent it."

TEACHING OF THE SCRIBES.

The evil of the teaching of the scribes did not consist so much in its direct falsity, as in its perversion of the truth; not so much in promulgating new and erroneous principles, as in making a wrong application of the old and the right. The most wicked and dangerous doctrines assumed, in their system, the form of necessary inferences from the laws laid down by God himself. Thus, God had said, "Thou shalt love thy neighbour as thyself;" and they drew from this command, the sinful inference that they might lawfully and properly hate their enemies. God enjoined alms-giving, fasting, and prayer, as *duties;* hence, they concluded that these were *meritorious services*, deserving the approbation of man and the favour of heaven. Moses permitted divorce, in certain cases, but required that a writing of divorcement should be given to the cast-off wife. This was done for her benefit, security, and protection. But they inferred that the giving of this writing was all that was necessary to legalize divorce, and to justify the husband in his desertion of his wife. So that through their perverted construction of the Mosaic law, that which was intended for the protection of the poor woman, became the source of the greatest prejudice to her. God had said, "ye shall not swear by my name falsely." They laid all the stress upon the word "*name*," and hence, concluded that they might innocently use any form of oath which did not involve the dreadful name of Jehovah. The rule for the magistrate, in the redress of injuries, wantonly and maliciously inflicted, was, "an eye for an eye, and a tooth for a tooth." But they deduced from this rule for the *executive officer*, the right of *private individuals* to retaliate blow for blow, and wrong for wrong. And so, in regard to every other law and principle of justice, they perverted their plain and obvious meaning, put a false gloss or false construction upon them, or drew a false conclusion from them. Heretics, in every age of the world, have pursued identically the same course as that of the Scribes in the days of our Saviour. Heresy has ever crept stealthily in, not boldly proclaiming its infamous doctrines, but twisting and perverting the truth, making wrong applications of, and drawing false inferences from the law of God, either written in the heart and conscience, or else in his own Book Divine. It is this insidious approach of error, and its insidious perversions, that make it so potent and so pernicious. Nature itself teaches us that perverted good is the worst form of evil. The noble stream, confined within its natural channel, blesses and fertilizes the valley through which it flows; but when it has broken over its boundaries, it becomes the desolating flood—the messenger of God's wrath and vengeance. The fire on the hearth is among the cherished memories in all after life, of the dear old homestead. But that same element, when changed from its natural use of comfort and utility, is one of the most fearful agents of ruin and destruction. Who has not enjoyed the fresh, invigorating breath of the morning, and the cool, refreshing breeze of evening? But who does not shrink back with terror upon witnessing the ravages of the storm and the tornado? Who does not fear the air he breathes, when every gale comes loaded with miasma, or tainted with pestilence? How soothing and how nourishing is the breast of the healthful mother to her helpless babe, and how injurious and pernicious is it when she is sickly and diseased? And if we turn from the physical to the moral world, we find the same evil consequences flowing from perverted good. What is pride but inordinate self-esteem; fear, but exaggerated prudence; anger, but excess of the principle of self-protection; depraved inclinations, but perverted natural appetites? And just as the best of medicines become the worst of poisons, when given in excess or wrongly applied, so the passions and emotions implanted in our bosoms for wise and good purposes, become sources of sin and evil, when allowed to become inordinate, or to be misdirected. The bitterest hate is that which results from estranged affection. No enemy is so malignant as the alienated friend. Hence the hatred of the sinner for holiness and God. The faculties which were given him, in order that he might glorify his Creator, have been perverted and prostituted to selfish indulgences and unholy pursuits. Hence he hates the Being who gave him the powers which he has abused and misapplied. And just in proportion to the vigour of his natural endowments, and the extent of his attainments, will be the depth of his rancour and enmity towards God. The greatest nuisance to society, and the greatest foe to all that is noble, good, and true, is the man of high and cultivated intellect, who has perverted his powers from the service of God, and consecrated them to the world, the flesh, and the devil. The enlargement of the mind by reading, observation, and reflection, when it fails to deepen reverence for God, and abhorrence for sin, is sure to enlarge the capacity for all manner of wickedness and crime.

The formalism of the Scribes and Pharisees resulted from their perversion of the teaching of Moses and the prophets. With these illustrious teachers, certain duties were expected to flow necessarily from love to God and love to man, and to be the spontaneous actings out of the dictates of the renewed heart. The outward act was right, because the inner principle was right. The fruit was good, because the tree was good. Hence the great thing with "the inspired men of old" was to have all sound within, that all might be sound without. The Scribes and Pharisees perverted all this. They looked at the act, and cared nothing for the motive that prompted to the act. Good deeds, instead of being regarded as evidences of holiness of heart, were regarded as *holiness itself*. And thus, if the walls were whited, they cared not for the rottenness and dead men's bones within the sepulchre. Naturally then, they cared more for rites and ceremonies than for the breathings of the soul after God. Naturally then, they thought more of formal observances than of the hungering and thirsting of the soul after righteousness. And so the religion taught by the Scribes and illustrated by the Pharisees, was a stupid formalism. It was doubtless adorned by many seemingly good deeds, but these all were prompted by vain, selfish, and unholy motives. It may have had much external loveliness, but this was only the hectic glow of health on the cheek, while disease and corruption were preying on the vitals within.

TEACHING OF OUR SAVIOUR.

We will only venture to notice a few of the marked peculiarities of our Saviour's instruction. First: The most remarkable characteristic of this teaching was, no doubt, that which most impressed the auditory, viz. the power and authority with which it was uttered. He set aside and pronounced false the traditions of the elders, and the doctrines which had been received so long as infallibly true; and the only reason that he deigned to give for so doing, was his own declaration that they were wrong. He put his own "but I say unto you" above all the commandments of the most revered teachers and authoritative doctors of the law. This calm assumption of power and authority, instead of exciting the indignation of his hearers, seems only to have astonished them. Doubtless, there was a majesty in his manner, and a divine energy in the tones of his voice, which awed them into silence, and hushed their murmuring at the boldness of his words. The lips that spake were those of God manifest in the flesh, and their utterances must have thrilled upon the ears of the assembled multitude.

Second: The personality of his remarks must have produced a powerful effect upon men accustomed to the cold, tame, and lifeless teaching of the Scribes. He did not speak to the crowd, but to each individual in the crowd; and every one present must have felt himself personally addressed. There is no one word directed to the whole assembly; "you," "ye," "your," "their," "thee," and "thine," are the words employed. There is no dealing in generalities, all is particular, pointed, and pungent. There is no vague hinting at false teachers; the Scribes and Pharisees are designated by name. There is no indefinite reference to the errors taught; they are plainly mentioned, denounced, and refuted. There is no ambiguous allusion to sins of practice; their nature and character are unmistakably defined. The whole discourse is earnest, faithful, and solemn, and well calculated to alarm the conscience, and to drive the sinner from his refuge of lies to the only Ark of hope and safety.

Third: The spiritual nature of the sermon. It recognizes the great truth that holiness in the soul makes holiness in the life. Hence the right heart, the right motive, the right principle, the right opinion;

these are the things enjoined and insisted upon, to produce right conduct and right deeds. It lays the axe at the root of the evil. It shows that the sinful thought causes the sinful act. It teaches that there may be adultery of the soul as well as of the body. It reminds us that God sees in secret, and scrutinizes the secret purpose, as well as the outward manifestation. It makes his glory the ultimate object of all religious worship. It requires love to him to be the foundation of all virtue. His righteousness is to be the first thing sought. His honour is to be the paramount consideration in every religious duty, in every secular pursuit and engagement. Finally, it builds a temple to his praise upon the rock Christ—the corner-stone, elect, precious, tried.

Fourth: The simplicity of the style and language. This wonderful sermon, with all its sublimity, depth, power, and comprehensiveness, is so simple that a child can understand it. There is no pomp of diction, no straining after effect, no rhetorical flourish, no extravagant figure, no wild allusion, no fanciful comparison. It is clothed in the plainest words; it draws its illustrations from objects familiar to all, and understood by all. The most unlettered peasant can grasp its meaning, the wisest philosopher can never exhaust it. The most careless reader can see its beauty, the most attentive student will fail to discover all its loveliness. Its richness, sweetness, fulness, adaptation to the wants and condition of man, may be partially understood now; eternity alone can reveal them in all their perfection. Is it strange then, that those who heard the first time this discourse, so simple and yet so sublime, were powerfully impressed by it? Is it strange that they were astonished and awed by it? If we, coldly reading it at the distance of so many centuries, can find no language wherewith to express our admiration, what must have been the emotions of those who heard the living, animated speaker, and that speaker the Son of God, the Saviour of the world? We can form no conception of their sensations, but we can, in the sincerity of our heart, echo back the words spoken on another, and most probably on this occasion also, "*Never man spake like this man.*"

THE END.

www.ingramcontent.com/pod-product-compliance
Lightning Source LLC
LaVergne TN
LVHW010225110826
845151LV00004B/1185
9781425527068